Saggistica 27

GARIBALDI M. LAPOLLA
A Study of His Novels

Champlain, New York

GARIBALDI M. LAPOLLA
A Study of His Novels

Steven J. Belluscio

BORDIGHERA PRESS

Library of Congress Control Number: 2017955425

Cover Art:
Park scene watercolor
Garibaldi M. Lapolla Papers
Historical Society of Pennsylvania
Philadelphia

Title Page Photo:
Garibaldi M. Lapolla Papers
Historical Society of Pennsylvania
Philadelphia

© 2017 by Steven J. Belluscio

All rights reserved. Parts of this book may be reprinted only by written permission from the author, and may not be reproduced for publication in book, magazine, or electronic media of any kind, except for purposes of literary review by critics.

Printed in the United States.

Published by
BORDIGHERA PRESS
John D. Calandra Italian American Institute
25 West 43rd Street, 17th Floor
New York, NY 10036

SAGGISTICA 27
ISBN 978-1-59954-125-9

Acknowledgements

I would like to thank Borough of Manhattan Community College/CUNY for awarding me the Faculty Publication Grant that allowed the completion of this book. I would also like to thank Dean Anthony J. Tamburri of the John D. Calandra Italian American Institute, Nick Grosso of Bordighera Press, and Kendra Millis of Millis Indexing for their invaluable assistance with the preparation of the manuscript. I should also acknowledge the superior staff at the Historical Society of Pennsylvania, Philadelphia, for their invaluable assistance with the Garibaldi M. Lapolla Papers and for granting me permission to use the images found herein. I'm grateful to Rutgers University Press for allowing me to use the chronology and the parts of the introduction that were originally published in my edited reprint of *The Grand Gennaro*, by Garibaldi M. Lapolla. Many thanks are extended to Paul M. Lapolla (1919-2012), Mark Lapolla, and Joann Lapolla for spending many hours talking with me about Garibaldi M. Lapolla and for granting me permission to use his work in this manuscript. I would like to show appreciation for the support of my colleagues at Borough of Manhattan Community College/CUNY, especially Professors Maria Enrico, Frank Elmi, and Joyce Harte. Also, I would like to thank Bordighera Press for its interest in this project and for all it does for Italian American studies. Finally, I would like to thank my wife, children, and parents.

Contents

Chronology   v

Introduction   xi

1. Garibaldi M. Lapolla's *The Fire in the Flesh*   1
   Desire and Italian-American Art

2. The Cactus Blooms   43
   Miss Rollins in Love and Italian-American Pedagogical Literature

3. Making America   77
   Garibaldi M. Lapolla's The Grand Gennaro

Bibliography   109

Index   127

Chronology

1888   Garibaldi Mario Lapolla is born April 5 in Rapolla, Basilicata, province of Potenza, Italy, to Biagio Oreste Lapolla and Marie Nicola Buonvicino. In honor of his grandfather's Italian nationalism, he is named after Giuseppe Garibaldi (1807–1882), the George Washington of the modern Italian nation.

1890   Immigrates to New York City with his parents. Over the next decade, over 650,000 of his fellow Italians would follow suit.

1891   Eleven Italians are lynched in New Orleans in connection with the unsolved murder of Police Chief David Hennessy.

1898   Spanish-American War.

1910   Earns A.B. at Columbia University. Begins his public school career teaching English at DeWitt Clinton High School, Manhattan, New York, where he remains for more than a decade, with an interruption for World War I military service.

1912   Earns A.M. at Columbia University after writing a thesis on British romanticist Percy Bysshe Shelley (1792–1822) entitled "Shelley and the Political Parties of His Day."

1914–18   World War I. Italian immigration stopped.

1917–18   Enlists in the U.S. Army and is stationed at Fort Ontario, Oswego, New York. Mess sergeant for the hospital. Meets Nurse Margaret McCormick, whom he marries soon after. Signs a letter published in the *New Republic* on May 26, 1917, arguing that conscientious objectors be allowed to serve non-combat roles in the military. Is transferred to Washington, D.C. Promoted to sergeant first class.

1918   Marries Margaret McCormick.

1919   Son Paul McCormick is born February 11.

1921   Emergency Quota Act severely limits immigration from southern and eastern European countries.

1922   Summoned by the Advisory Council on the Qualification of Teachers, formed by Frank Graves, state commissioner of education, to determine the patriotism of teachers in New York State. Lapolla is questioned about the 1917 *New Republic* letter he signed. Son Mark Orestes is born February 17.

1924   Immigration Act of 1924 enacted, an even harsher version of the 1921 law. It prohibits Asian immigration entirely.

1925   Publication of F. Scott Fitzgerald novel, *The Great Gatsby*.

1926–30   Chairman of Thomas Jefferson High School English Department.

1927   On August 23, Ferdinando Nicola Sacco (b. 1891) and Bartolomeo Vanzetti (b. 1888), two Italian anarchists, are executed for the 1920 murder of two pay clerks in South Braintree, Massachusetts. Given the antiradical sentiment of the court, many argue they did not receive a fair trial.

1927–32 Principal of Thomas Jefferson Summer High School.

1928 Serves as judge in a Brooklyn Borough high school finals for the National Oratorical Contest on the Constitution.

1929 Publishes *Better High School English through Tests and Drills* with Kenneth W. Wright at Noble & Noble. Edits with poet and literary critic Mark Van Doren *A Junior Anthology of World Poetry*, published by Albert & Charles Boni, and praised highly in the *New York Times*. Divorces Margaret McCormick.

1930–34 Principal of New York Public School 112.

1930 Exchanges letters with famed teacher and educational theorist Leonard Covello, refusing to allow the latter to use the as yet unpublished *The Fire and the Flesh* (then with the working title "La Dantone") as a sociological document for a study of Italian Americans because "it ain't no such beast."

1931 Publishes *The Fire in the Flesh* at the Vanguard Press to generally positive reviews in *Books* and the *New York Times*.

1932 Publishes *Miss Rollins in Love* at the Vanguard Press. Receives lukewarm review from the *New York Times*.

1934 Marries Priscilla Sherman. Is featured (with other Italian American authors) in *Gazzetta del Popolo*.

1935–53 Principal of New York Public School 174.

1935 Publishes *The Grand Gennaro* at the Vanguard Press to acclaim in the *New Republic*, the *New York Times*, Books, the *Boston Transcript*, *Review of Reviews*, and the *Saturday Review of Literature*.

1937   Publishes *Required Grammar in the New York City Public School* at Noble & Noble. Interviewed on WEVD New York for a radio program about overcrowding in city schools.

1938   Speaks on June 29 at the conference of the National Council of Teachers of English and criticizes the tendency to insist upon a "puritanical type of speech" no one actually uses and to reinforce it through teaching of grammar and usage.

1939   Publication of Pietro di Donato novel *Christ in Concrete*.

1939–45 World War II. Over one million Italian Americans serve in the armed forces. About 250 Italian Americans, 11,000 German Americans, and 100,000 Japanese Americans are interned for reasons of "national security."

1945   In February, son Mark Orestes, trained as an Army Air Corps flight officer reported missing in action over Brod, Yugoslavia, after completing eighteen missions and receiving the Air Medal. His death was confirmed eleven months later.

1946   Serves on a Teacher-Author Committee of New York City school and college instructors to protest Board of Education bylaw requiring textbook authors to turn over royalties.

1950   Unsuccessfully brings action against the New York City Board of Education in favor of uniform pay for principals of all city schools, elementary, junior, and senior.

1953   Publishes and illustrates *Italian Cooking for the American Kitchen and The Mushroom Cookbook* at W.

Funk. The former is praised and widely publicized by reviews and interviews in publications such as the *New York Times*, the *San Francisco News*, *Il Progresso Italo-Americano*, the *Chicago American*, and the *Sunday Herald*.

1954   Dies in his sixty-fifth year on January 13 at Mount Sinai Hospital after a massive stroke. His death is mourned and career celebrated by colleagues, administrators, students, and parents. The Parent Teacher Association donates to Public School 174 a plaque lauding Lapolla as "Educator, Leader, and Friend."

1965   Immigration Act of 1965 overturns Immigration Act of 1924.

Introduction

When Thomas J. Ferraro declared Italian-American writing "one of the better kept literary secrets of [the twentieth] century," he had in mind Garibaldi M. Lapolla, among other authors.[1] In their detailed and sensitive treatment of everyday life in early twentieth-century Italian Harlem, Lapolla's three published novels—*The Fire in the Flesh* (1931), *Miss Rollins in Love* (1932), and *The Grand Gennaro* (1935)—form a cornerstone of early Italian-American fiction for readers familiar with the likes of Silvio Villa, Giuseppe Cautela, Louis Forgione, Frances Winwar, John Fante, Mari Tomasi, Pietro di Donato, Guido d'Agostino, and Jerre Mangione. However, Garibaldi M. Lapolla's writing has not garnered nearly the attention it deserves despite his renown among scholars of Italian-American literature, the similarity of his fiction to that of canonical ethnic writers such as Abraham Cahan and Anzia Yezierska, and the recent entry into the canon of other Italian-American fiction writers (such as Pietro di Donato and John Fante). To be sure, one obvious reason is unavailability. While Lapolla's novels were generally well reviewed—especially *The Grand Gennaro*, considered to be his best work—they soon went out of print. And despite an Arno Press resurrection of his first and last novels in 1975, Garibaldi M. Lapolla's name continues to remain in undeserved obscurity; he could very well be the best kept secret of Italian-American literature.

---

1 Ferraro, "Ethnicity in the Marketplace," 398.

Teacher, Soldier, Writer

Born April 5, 1888, in Rapolla, Basilicata, Province of Potenza, Italy, to Biagio Oreste Lapolla and Marie Nicola Lapolla (née Buonvicino), Garibaldi Mario Lapolla (his given name reflecting the Italian patriotism of his paternal grandfather) left Italy and immigrated to New York City with his parents in 1890 before age two. He would lose his mother at age nine.[2] An exceptional student in public school as a child, Lapolla attended Columbia University, earning a B.A. in 1910 and an M.A. in 1912, after completing a thesis on British romantic poet Percy Bysshe Shelley.[3] In 1910, Lapolla began teaching English at DeWitt Clinton High School, then located in Manhattan, where he left a great impression on his students, including Mortimer Adler, who would become one of America's most celebrated philosophers and public intellectuals of the twentieth century.[4] Thus began Lapolla's rich, productive, and lifelong career as an educator and educational theorist — a career interrupted only by military service during World War I in which he "held every position from buck private to cook to lecturer on personal prophylaxis to sergeant to lieutenant of artillery."[5]

From 1917 to 1918, Lapolla was stationed at Fort Ontario, Oswego, New York, where, after an "early [. . .] career [. . .] underscored by black marks" in which "he seemed temperamentally incapable of complying with regulations," "he

---

2 Luisa, 1; Peragallo, 138; Marazzi, "King of Harlem," 190, 207.
3 Oliver, "Beyond Ethnicity," 6; Hornsby, e-mail message to Belluscio, October 2, 2007. Lapolla's degrees were granted by Columbia University, not Columbia Teachers College, as has been erroneously assumed.
4 Adler, 29.
5 From the book jacket of the Vanguard Press edition of *The Fire in the Flesh* (1931), Oversized Folder 1, MSS 64, Garibaldi M. Lapolla Papers, Historical Society of Pennsylvania, Philadelphia.

disciplined himself to become a good soldier."⁶ As mess sergeant, he nurtured what would become a lifelong passion and what had been a family tradition of sorts: his father had owned restaurants in Montreal, Quebec, and New York, and was known to claim descent from "a long line of cooks" dating back to Ancient Rome.⁷ While a soldier in Flower Unit N, Post Hospital No. 5, Fort Ontario, Lapolla met his future wife, Nurse Margaret McCormick, whom he married in 1918 and with whom he conceived two sons: Paul McCormick (born February 11, 1919) and Mark Oreste (born Feburary 17, 1922).⁸ Lapolla also served on the Associate Board of the *Ontario Post* newspaper and wrote for it, taught in the fort's school, played guard and tackle for its football team, and worked as a chaplain's assistant before he was transferred to Washington and eventually promoted to Sergeant First Class.⁹

After his successful tenure at DeWitt Clinton High School, where he taught on the faculty alongside famed educational theorist and Italian-American activist Leonard Covello, Lapolla served as chairman of the Thomas Jefferson High School English Department from 1926 to 1930 and principal of the Thomas Jefferson Summer High School from 1927 to 1932. In 1929, Lapolla's first marriage ended in divorce; in 1934, he married Priscilla Sherman, a fellow faculty member. From 1930 to 1934, Lapolla was principal of Public School 112, and from 1934 to his death in 1954, principal of Public School 174.¹⁰

---

6 "Editor's Notebook."
7 Garibaldi M. Lapolla, *Italian Food for the American Kitchen*, ix.
8 Lear, e-mail message to Belluscio, October 1, 2007; Ancestry.com; Paul Lapolla, telephone interview by Belluscio, June 25, 2007.
9 *Ontario Post*, September 22, 1917; September 29, 1917; December 8, 1917; April 20, 1918; May 25, 1918; June 1, 1918.
10 Blackburn, 1-2; *New York Times*, January 14, 1954, 29.

Lapolla fought for social justice throughout his life, even running "for every office from Alderman to Congressman on the Socialist ticket" before World War I.[11] Unwilling to sell short immigrant students, he campaigned endlessly for more intelligent, student-centered pedagogical practices in the tradition of John Dewey and a more pragmatic approach to teaching English grammar, rankling school administrators but advocating what would eventually become educational orthodoxy. In keeping with his democratic educational vision, Lapolla also challenged Board of Education by-laws requiring textbook authors to turn over royalties to the school district and fought for uniform pay for principals of all city schools.[12] This fighting spirit often got him into trouble. For example, in 1922, he was interrogated by the Advisory Council on the Qualification of Teachers—a by-product of the 1919 Joint Legislative Committee to Investigate Seditious Activities (also known as the Lusk Committee)—about his co-signed letter printed in the May 26, 1917, issue of the *New Republic*, which argued that conscientious objectors ought to be allowed to serve non-combat roles in the military during World War I and, more broadly, that there ought to be "a social setting within America sufficiently hospitable to all conscientious objectors."[13] Upton Sinclair would later relish the irony of Lapolla, "an artillery officer" during the war, "now . . . sitting on the bench, humbly waiting his turn to be browbeaten."[14] While Lapolla escaped the investigation unscathed, he would be unable to avoid similar controversy in the future.

---

11 This quotation, taken from the book jacket of *The Fire in the Flesh* (1931), is qtd. in Blackburn, 2.
12 "Teachers Oppose Loss of Royalties," 7; "Principals Lose Pay Case," 12.
13 "Teachers Secretly Quizzed on Loyalty," 18; Thomas, et al., letter to the editor, 109
14 Sinclair, 84.

As principal of Public School 174 in Brooklyn in the early 1950s, Lapolla vigorously defended teachers persecuted by the House Un-American Activities Committee, arguing that they should be judged not for their beliefs but, rather, their ability in the classroom. "Aren't we, in fact," Lapolla wrote, "chasing a phantom that, in a more reasonable period, we would recognize and admit as such?"[15] Throughout his educational career, Lapolla remained aggressively committed to winning justice for students, teachers, and administrators and maintaining quality in education.

As an English specialist, Lapolla taught "grammar, American literature, English literature, poetry, Shakespeare, and remedial English."[16] Frequently dissatisfied with the status quo of English pedagogy, Lapolla published textbooks designed to teach English grammar more practically and to deliver an appreciation of literature to young students. During his career, he penned *Better High School English* (1929) and *Required Grammar in the New York Public Schools* (1937) to serve the former purpose and co-edited with Mark Van Doren *The Junior Anthology of World Poetry* (1929) to serve the latter. Lapolla was also interested in educating the general public about the delights of the Italian cuisine he had grown up enjoying and masterfully learning to prepare. In 1953, he published *Italian Cooking for the American Kitchen*, designed to help Americans learn the variety of Italian cooking; that same year, he also published *The Mushroom Cookbook*. Lapolla also left behind a wealth of unpublished writings—essays, poems, plays, short stories, a novel titled "Jerry," and other unfinished manuscripts.

---

15 Garibaldi M. Lapolla, "Letter in Answer to Dr. Lefkowitz about So-Called Communist Teachers," 3-5.
16 Blackburn, 2.

The unifying thread of most of Lapolla's written work — his textbooks, his cookbooks, and his novels — is the continuous negotiation between Italian and American cultures. His textbooks were designed in part with the Italian immigrant student in mind and the concern of how best to serve them in the American public school system. His cookbooks attempted to teach an American audience about Italian food and thereby provide an entrée into Italian history, culture, and geography: as Americans learned to prepare and appreciate Italian cuisine, these so-called foreigners in their midst would come to seem less foreign. Finally, his novels used turn-of-the-century East Harlem as a fictional staging ground for the oft-troubled coexistence of Italian ancestry and American dreams. All the while, *Professore* Lapolla is the patient and compassionate pedagogue, challenging his student — the reader — to grow beyond the limitations of prior experience.

Lapolla traveled widely during his lifetime throughout North America, South America, and Europe, including his native Italy. Lapolla was an avid artist; many of his pencil sketches, pen and ink drawings, and water colors — mostly urban scenes, rural pastorals, portraits, and still lifes — serve as a record of the people and places he encountered at home and abroad. Lapolla even supplied the pen and ink drawings of various foods for *Italian Cooking for the American Kitchen*. An expert letter writer, Lapolla infused his correspondence with wry humor and keen wit, both high- and lowbrow. He would regale his reader with evocative accounts of his New York surroundings before matter-of-factly addressing the main subject matter of the letter. His letters to younger son Mark Oreste Lapolla while the latter served in Foggia, Italy, as an Army Air Forces flight officer during World War II are ample evidence of this. In these letters to "Oreste," Lapolla discourses about

Italian language, geography, and culture; the progress of the war; and the mood of Americans back on the homefront. Of themselves, these letters are little gems of geopolitics, cultural criticism, and homespun wisdom.[17] Some of the best of these letters were returned, for Mark Lapolla went missing in action over Brod, Yugoslavia, while flying a mission during February 1945. On January 5, 1946, he was reported to have been killed there.[18] An emotional man, Lapolla took his son's death very hard, and during his 1953 trip to Italy, he visited Oreste's gravesite with his wife Priscilla, writing in his trip diary, "I couldn't have come here and not done it."[19]

When Garibaldi M. Lapolla died of a massive stroke on January 13, 1954, at the age of sixty-five, Priscilla received an outpouring of condolences for "Gari," as he was affectionately known, from colleagues and friends throughout his life and career praising his qualities as an educator, intellectual, artist, and fellow human. The Parent Teacher Association donated a plaque to New York Public School 174 lauding Lapolla as an "Educator, Leader, and Friend." Although he died much too young, he had the great fortune of being remembered, and celebrated, by friends and acquaintances for all the many things he had accomplished.

"Method Realistic, But Intent Romantic"

Garibaldi M. Lapolla's reputation as a novelist, however, would be neglected until the 1980s, when scholarship began to recognize his talent and importance as "East Harlem's nov-

---

17 Garibaldi M. Lapolla to Mark O. Lapolla, returned letters, December 25, 1944; January 7, 1945; January 15, 1945; January 31, 1945; February 6, 1945.
18 "Missing Flight Officer Now Is Reported Killed," 30.
19 Paul Lapolla, telephone interview by Belluscio, November 11, 2007. Garibaldi M. Lapolla, European trip diary, 1953.

elist"—or, at least, Italian Harlem's novelist.[20] Critics have rightly attributed Lapolla's obscurity in part to his refusal to accede to the aesthetic trends of the 1930s: high modernism and proletarian literature.[21] In course lecture notes, it is clear that while Lapolla was by no means opposed to the literary experimentation of the early twentieth century, he disliked the use of "pyrotechnical coloring and devices" for their own sake; and while Lapolla was himself a socialist, he dismissively refers to proletarian literature as "propaganda" "mainly concerned with revealing the life of worker-classes as they are allegedly developing a historic class-consciousness."[22]

Furthermore, Lapolla celebrated what he called the "newer romanticis[m]" of contemporary authors who "have held to the notion that the novel was made to please, that factual scenes immediate to the readers' experience are not the inevitable material of the novel, that readers are still interested in the carefully organized plot, in remote peoples and times, in themes that have no bearing on modern conditions save in a large way, that propaganda for any cause is not the purpose of fiction." Lapolla admired Pearl Buck's writing for providing "pictures which please by their combination of the familiar in human nature against a background of the unfamiliar," her "method realistic, but intent romantic."[23]

This description goes a long way toward explaining Lapolla's own aesthetic approach. While his fictions are rich

---

20 Orsi, *The Madonna of 115th Street*, 22. Richard A. Meckel considers Lapolla to be "as good as many of the better known ethnic/immigrant social realists of the 1930s and 1940s" ("A Reconsideration," 127); and Lawrence J. Oliver claims, "outside of Puzo and Pietro di Donato, no writer has so skillfully portrayed the marble beneath the mud, to use Nathaniel Hawthorne's expression, of the Italian-American immigrant experience ("'Great Equalizer' or 'Cruel Stepmother'?": 116).
21 Marazzi, "King of Harlem," 191; Meckel, 128.
22 Garibaldi M. Lapolla, "The American Novel."
23 Ibid.

with the realistic specifics of place and people—East Harlem and the Italians who once lived there—the pastness of these very specifics lends them, even from the perspective of the 1930s, the luster of historical romance. Furthermore, Lapolla frequently imbues his settings with firelight, moonlight, shadowplay, and religious iconography, elements more typical of Nathaniel Hawthorne or Edgar Allan Poe than William Dean Howells or Henry James. The traditional Southern Italian folk beliefs fictionalized by Lapolla—with their fascinating interplay of Christian providence, saint worship, Marianism, and occult mysticism—further add to the otherworldly romanticism of the novels. Furthermore, Lapolla's novels feature characters who attempt to rise above their sordid urban surroundings—the literary content of realism—toward a romantic, transcendental plane of spiritual and—given the recurrence of the artist figure in all three of his works—artistic fulfillment.[24] Lapolla's romantic realism was anticipated as early in 1911 in his Columbia M.A. thesis "Shelley and the Political Parties of His Day," in which he praises British romantic poet Percy Bysshe Shelley not for having the political beliefs of a wild-eyed romantic idealist but rather for having "a curiously balanced compound of high-minded aspirations and common sense demands."[25] Romantic "visionary" though Shelley may have been, "his intentions were always to transform his intellectual and emotional interest into practical devices."[26]

---

24 As Lawrence J. Oliver writes, "Lapolla's novels display the ethical idealism—the belief that the people can rise above corrupting and degrading influences to a higher moral plane—that marks [. . .] romantic literature in general. Indeed, if a label must be applied to Lapolla's novels, the most appropriate would be that coined by Frank Norris, 'romances of the commonplace'" ("Beyond Ethnicity," 18-19).
25 Garibaldi M. Lapolla, "Shelley and the Political Parties of His Day," 41.
26 Ibid., 12.

Writing the Domus

In his study of faith in Italian Harlem, *The Madonna of 115th Street*, Robert Anthony Orsi writes, "There is an iconography of the streets in dense urban communities like Italian Harlem: the street is a text composed by the people, though their composition is shaped and constrained by the social and economic facts of their lives. The people of Italian Harlem lived on the streets almost as much as they lived in their homes: the streets became extensions of their homes. The street life of Italian Harlem was dense with symbols that adumbrated the inner structures of community life and the inner meanings of the people's lives."[27] As Italian Harlem's author, an artist who worked with these very "symbols," "structures," and "meanings," Garibaldi M. Lapolla gave voice to one aspect of lived experience in a neighborhood with a rich, multinational and multiethnic past. After having spent most of the seventeenth and eighteenth centuries under Dutch and British control, by the turn of the twentieth century, Harlem was primarily Irish and German American.[28] The first of the southern- and eastern-European "new immigrants" to come to Harlem, the Italians by 1910 were its second largest ethnic group.[29] In its 1920s, 30s, and 40s heyday, Italian Harlem stretched from 104th to 120th Streets at its southern and northern extremes and from Third Avenue to the East River at its western and eastern extremes.[30] It is mostly within this geographic periphery that Lapolla's fictions are set.

However, there is also a cultural periphery that Lapolla establishes, and that is arguably the *domus* described at length

---

27 Orsi, *The Madonna of 115th Street*, 33.
28 Sexton, 4-5.
29 Osofsky, 82; Sexton, 5.
30 Orsi, The Madonna of 115th Street, 17.

by Orsi. "The source of meaning and morals in Italian Harlem," the domus refers to the nuclear and extended families created by Italian immigrants and all the traditional values regarding culture, religion, ethics, and family inculcated therein.[31] "The center of their lives and culture," the domus was the means by which Italian immigrants compared themselves favorably to native-born and ethnic Americans alike.[32] Orsi tells us, "Two kinds of stories were popular on the streets and in the living rooms of Italian Harlem: tales of the doums in all its complexity, and tales of the Mafia. But the most popular tale of all combined the two genres. These were the stories [. . .] of the Mafia defending the domus."[33] While Lapolla says comparatively little about the Mafia—with the exception of gangster Paul Variglia in *The Fire in the Flesh*, false accusations against protagonist Donato Contini of involvement with organized crime in *Miss Rollins in Love*, and the gangster-like behavior of Agnese Dantone and Gennaro Accuci in *The Fire in the Flesh* and *The Grand Gennaro*, respectively—his fictions establish the Italian Harlem domus as a literary microcosm in which every human desire and conflict is possible.

While the literal meaning of the Latin *domus* as "house" or "home" may lend a kind of peace and stability to the word's connotative meaning, in reality, "[t]he domus in Italian Harlem was the scene of bitter conflict and profound struggle" between differing interpretations of its demands and utility.[34] Lapolla recreates an Italian Harlem that seems hermetically sealed off from the rest of the world as if in a snow globe. Still, it is not as if there is no "outside world" in Lapolla's

---

31   Ibid., 75.
32   Ibid., 77.
33   Ibid., 127.
34   Ibid., 108.

fiction. In his three published novels, non-Italian-American characters number greatly and sometimes figure prominently. However, when Italian-American characters find themselves in conflict with that "American" "outside world" — that land beyond the safe confines of the Italian Harlem domus — they generally find that they are really battling themselves, or other Italian Americans, who have in part internalized the values — *vis-à-vis* money, love, assimilation, education, and any number of concerns — of that outside world.

In part, this sense of seclusion is no doubt reflective of Italian Harlemites' notoriety for insularity — a product of southern Italians' oppression-fueled regionalism, often termed *campanilismo*, or the unwillingness to trust anyone from beyond the reach of the village church bell (*campana*).[35] Jonathan Gill goes so far as to call Italian Harlem "a city unto itself."[36] For readers, being able to view a broad range of human conflict and possibility within Lapolla's literary domus has the counterintuitive effect of making that domus seem not more foreign but rather more familiar. This effect is what Robert Viscusi has termed the "concentric history" of Italian-American literature, a variety of history writing in which ever-expanding circles of inclusive historical meaning are drawn and redrawn, first with the purpose of looking inward, and then with the purpose of moving outward "into the civic space of the United States."[37] Lapolla, in other words, writes of the relatively small circle of the Italian Harlem domus — a word that, especially for English speakers, itself connotes circularity — and as the concerns of the domus are revealed in all their universality, the circle extends outward.

---

35 Gurock, 50; Gambino, 71.
36 Gill, 335.
37 Viscusi, *Buried Caesars*, 131.

Garibaldi M. Lapolla as Italian-American Writer

Lapolla reworks themes that have long fascinated American writers, in particular the artistic, romantic soul encountering a vast, sprawling nature (i.e., Walt Whitman, Ralph Waldo Emerson, and Henry David Thoreau), even if, in Lapolla's case, "nature" turns out to be a vast, sprawling city! Lapolla also shows concern for the modern individual in his attempt to come to terms with the mores of a rapidly urbanizing society (i.e., Henry James, William Dean Howells, Edith Wharton, and Kate Chopin). However, usually when we encounter Lapolla in critical literature, we encounter him as an "Italian-American writer," so it is important to take time to consider what that might mean.

Several critics have attempted to produce overarching theories of Italian-American literature, or at least Italian-American narrative. In order to describe Garibaldi M. Lapolla, it would help to situate him within the most influential of these theories. The earliest comprehensive theory appeared in *The Italian-American Novel: A Document of the Interaction of Two Cultures* (1974), by Rose Basile Green. As the subtitle indicates, Green believes that Italian-American autobiographies and novels dramatize the "social conflict" of Italians and Italian Americans with Americans and American culture. Green traces this conflict through seven stages of the Italian-American narrative, the first non-fictional and the remaining six fictional: 1) autobiography, 2) "early impact," 3) "the need for assimilation," 4) "the revulsion into non-Italian-American themes," 5) "the counter-revulsion, a return to old sources," 6) "the branching of an Italian culture rooted in American soil," and 7) "the contemporary period."[38] Green places Garibaldi

---

38 Green, 23-24.

M. Lapolla in the "early impact" phase of Italian-American narrative, "the period of explanatory narratives describing the early problems of the first encounter of the Italian culture with that of established America."[39] However, it would not be a stretch to place Lapolla within "the need for assimilation" phase, in which the writer presents "an analysis of Italo-American life (as a co-culture) in communities separate from the national culture."[40] Lapolla's characters dwell within distinct Italian-American communities and often confront dilemmas created by a felt need for assimilation. Lapolla arguably writes in a middle ground between "early impact," which manifests itself when he describes the first post-migration experiences of immigrant characters, and "need for assimilation," which manifests itself when he describes problems encountered by characters not as individuals but rather as members of an ethnic community.

In 1996, Fred L. Gardaphé articulated a three-stage theory of Italian-American prose in *Italian Signs, American Streets: The Evolution of Italian American Narrative*. Gardaphé bases his categories of the Italian-American narrative—the poetic, mythic, and philosophic modes—upon Enlightenment philosopher Giambattista Vico's three stages of culture: the Age of Gods, the Age of Heroes, and the Age of Man.[41] Writers of the poetic mode, such as Rosa Cavalleri, Pascal d'Angelo, and Constantine Panunzio, write autobiographically of their very first experiences as recent immigrants to the United States. Generally speaking, these narratives are optimistic in tone and uncritical of the American culture to which its authors adjust. Writers of the mythic mode, such as John Fante, Pietro

---

39   Ibid., 23.
40   Ibid.
41   Gardaphé, *Italian Signs, American Streets*, 15-16.

di Donato, Jerre Mangione, Mari Tomasi, Tina de Rosa, and Helen Barolini, move away from the strict autobiography of the poetic mode and develop characters less likely to accept passively their fate as Italian Americans. Writers of the philosophic mode, such as Don de Lillo, Gilbert Sorrentino, and Mary Caponegro, demonstrate their passage into the American mainstream by adopting its literary avant-gardisms and employing Italian signs only occasionally and often parodically at that. Garibaldi M. Lapolla would likely be placed within the mythic mode of this schema because his Italian characters often find themselves in conflict with American values, if not with Americans themselves.

In 1998, Anthony J. Tamburri's *A Semiotic of Ethnicity: In (Re)Cognition of the Italian/American Writer* establishes a connection between Gardaphé's three stages of Italian-American narrative and Daniel Aaron's three stages (local colorist, militant protester, and American) of the ethnic-American writer as described in his 1964 essay "The Hyphenate Writer and American Letters." Tamburri further establishes *italianità* ("Italianness") as the defining textual feature of Italian-American literature, which he separates into three groups based upon philosopher Charles Peirce's concepts of cognitive "firstness," "secondness," and "thirdness": expressive, comparative, and synthetic.[42] While an expressive writer like Tony Ardizzone deals in the immediate "feelings" of Italian immigrants like writers of Gardaphé's poetic mode, a comparative writer like Helen Barolini, whom we would place in Gardaphé's mythic mode, "sets up a distinct polarity between his/her cultural heritage and the dominant culture in that she attempts to construct a *sui generis* ethnic paradigm."[43]

---

42 Tamburri, *A Semiotic of Ethnicity*, 14.
43 Ibid., 13.

Meanwhile, like Gardaphé's philosophic mode writer, Tamburri's synthetic writer — for example, Giose Rimanelli — is capable of self-reflection and fashions a synthesis of ethnic and non-ethnic influences that advances Italian-American literature beyond the binarism of the comparative writers.[44] According to this understanding of Italian-American literary history, Lapolla would be classed as a comparative writer, for the conflicts that advance the plots of his novels pit Italian characters against American ideals and influences they do not always fully understand.

In 2002's *Writing with an Accent: Contemporary Italian American Women Writers*, Edvige Giunta argues that the titular accent is the defining feature of Italian-American literature. Analogous with Tamburri's use of *italianità*, "the word 'accent' [. . .] refer[s] to a series of elements — narrative, thematic, and linguistic — that, collectively, articulate the experience of living between cultures."[45] According to Giunta,

> A marker of difference, a vestige of otherness, an accent signals marginalization and separation. This is particularly true in the works of writers who have deliberately incorporated bilingualism in their writings as a political gesture through which to legitimize diversity and who proclaim that multilingualism is central to their experience as well as the North American cultural experience as a whole.[46]

While Lapolla would not have viewed his writing as a "political gesture" of any kind, it would be silly to dismiss the bilingual and multicultural components of his three published novels. Lapolla clearly did write — thematically, symbolically, and linguistically — with an accent, a fact that, as Joseph Scio-

---

44 Ibid.
45 Giunta, 2.
46 Ibid., 4.

rra would argue, "[i]n keeping with Giunta's conceptualization," requires us to "listen [. . .] with an accent as a means for understanding the variety of Italian-American vernacular expressivity."⁴⁷ For readers, listening, and by extension, reading with an accent is part of a double-edged approach that allows us to situate Lapolla's work both within a broader national tradition and the ethnic tradition we know as Italian-American literature.

Robert Viscusi, in 2006, published *Buried Caesars and Other Secrets of Italian American Writing*, which establishes the figurative "buried Caesar" as the defining feature of Italian-American written discourse. According to Viscusi, "Buried Caesars provide Italian Americans with a shared historical and cultural point of view." He argues further that "the secret culture of Italian Americans, like that of Italy itself, has to do with their attachment to the myth of Italian greatness in all its manifestations large and small."⁴⁸ Of course, these myths are by no means uncomplicated, and the claims to Italian greatness made by gutsy entrepreneurs like Agnese Dantone and Gennaro Accuci and passionate artists like Gino Birrichino, Giovanni Dantone, and Donato Contini cannot be understood without reference to the troubled Italian pasts and American futures each of these characters must negotiate.

In *By the Breath of Their Mouths: Narratives of Resistance in Italian America* (2010), Mary Jo Bona argues that Italian-American literature draws upon Italian America's "storytelling traditions" to recall its own "ancestral heritage" and to resist full assimilation.⁴⁹ A heralded public school principal during the years his novels were published, Lapolla's decidedly Ital-

---

47 Sciorra, "Introduction," 7.
48 Viscusi, *Buried Caesars*, 15.
49 Bona, 2.

ian-American narratives resisted a full identification with the dominant culture to which he could have plausibly laid claim. His novels also resisted prevailing American literary trends of Lapolla's day in spite of the fact that this may very well have contributed to their obscurity. As readers, we join the resistance, so to speak, when we read writers who, like Lapolla, have been long neglected by the critical mainstream.

Each chapter of the book that follows covers a different published novel in Garibaldi M. Lapolla's literary career. Chapter 1 explores the theme of desire in *The Fire in the Flesh* (1931), which documents the Dantone family's adjustment to life in urban Italian America. Next, chapter 2 reads *Miss Rollins in Love* (1932) as a cornerstone of Italian-American progressive pedagogical literature, whose non-Italian-American intellectual forefather John Dewey influenced a number of Italian-American educators, such as Angelo Patri, Leonard Covello, and Lapolla himself. Finally, chapter 3 examines the many facets of the leitmotif "making America" in what is generally accepted to be Lapolla's finest work, *The Grand Gennaro* (1935).

Garibaldi M. Lapolla's *The Fire in the Flesh*
Desire and Italian-American Art

In 1931, Garibaldi M. Lapolla published *The Fire in the Flesh*, the first of three Vanguard Press novels dealing with the adjustment of an immigrant family—in this case, the Dantones—to life in fin-de-siècle Italian Harlem. Early critical reception to the novel was mixed, to say the least. While a New York Times review gave the novel some left-handed praise— namely, that it "has an air of veracity which may be attributed to the background of the author," who is said to be "a gifted writer"—it also claimed that "the novel is marred by much material that should have been pruned away."[1]

And while Harriet Sampson of *New York Herald Tribune Books* praised Lapolla's characters as "real" and his fictional Little Italy as having been "drawn in detail with surprising honesty," she also judged the novel "to be overdramatic" with "too much flesh and blood."[2] An unpublished review written in 1932 praised the novel's atmosphere as "colorful and true to life" but considered the "situations" to be "exaggerated, and, at times, impossible." Still worse, the reviewer claims, "the novel lacks educational value" due to Lapolla's ostensibly unrealistic characterization and overemphasis upon "all that is sensual."[3] Later, in the posthumously published *Italian-American Authors and Their Contribution to American Literature* (1949), Olga Peragallo all but dismisses the novel

---

1 Review of *The Fire in the Flesh*, BR4.
2 Sampson, 16.
3 Todaro.

as "carnal and melodramatic."[4] More recent critics, however, have attempted to rehabilitate the novel's reputation. Rose Basile Green, writing from the perspective of American/Italian cultural interaction, says, "Although the plot is uneven in intensity, the book has educative value in its presentation of the Italian community of New York."[5] Lawrence J. Oliver, in three 1987 articles, gives the novel value in its treatment of American schools, Italian-American art, and Little Italy.[6] Then, in 2003, Martino Marazzi, in the most detailed reading of Lapolla's work to date, not unjustifiably considers *The Fire in the Flesh* as part of a steady novelistic progression leading up to l'opera maggiore, *The Grand Gennaro*, as he draws attention to the folkloric rootedness of the first novel, its narrative structure, and some variations on the theme suggested by the title.[7] However, *The Fire in the Flesh* has yet to be considered fully from the perspective of its unequivocal leitmotif desire, which is signaled by the evocative and suggestive title and is artfully figured throughout the text.

This paper will map the function of desire in *The Fire in the Flesh* and determine its moral, aesthetic, and artistic significance for Lapolla. While this chapter is decidedly *not* a psychoanalytic reading, it does rely upon principles drawn from Sigmund Freud, Jacques Lacan, and later theorists of narrative desire. First is the concept of need, which is said to be "constant" and instinctual—the most primal of human drives, which are divisible into life instincts (Eros) and death instincts (Thanatos).[8] Second is the concept of desire, which is

---

4 Peragallo, 140.
5 Green, 73.
6 Oliver, "Beyond Ethnicity," "'Great Equalizer' or 'Cruel Stepmother?'", and "The Re-Visioning of New York's Little Italies."
7 Marazzi, "I Due Re di Harlem," 538-41.
8 Clayton, 50; Freud, *Beyond the Pleasure Principle*, 55.

need's cognitive counterpart, and which comes into existence when need "enters history, language, culture, and society."[9] As we shall see, the nagging desires of Lapolla's characters are clearly products of their socioeconomic milieu. Third is the notion that desire is ultimately insatiable and "can never be satisfied by an object."[10]

The narrative economy of *The Fire in the Flesh* is not only enriched by the depiction of these desires; additionally, these desires give fuel to the narrative's very motion. Furthermore, Lapolla's rendering of desire has clear aesthetic and generic consequences that provide insight into his own motivations as a novelist. In the novel, Lapolla describes desire as an unavoidable, unquenchable, and biological fact of life: indeed, the "fire in the flesh" that motivates every human. The characters of *The Fire in the Flesh* are motivated by six basic and often interlinking desires: familial love, violence, erotic love, moneymaking and social mobility, power, and the transcendent. As they negotiate the minefield of desire in the novel, characters often find that one desire may lead directly, sometimes unexpectedly, to still another desire. And when they do not attempt to satisfy these desires—an endeavor that, by the very logic of desire, is destined for failure—they attempt to sublimate them through work and moneymaking, which simply produces yet another desire for more moneymaking. If desire is, as Lapolla would have it, unavoidable—if, in other words, we are always located in the middle ground between

---

9   Clayton, 50; Lacan, 311.
10 Clayton, 40; See also Lacan, 311; Butler, 381; Foster, 9; Bersani, *A Future for Astyanax*, 8; Bersani and Dutoit, 110-25; Deleuze and Guattari would concur that desire is indeed ongoing but view it as a continual "process of production" that creates all of reality and therefore creates also the need thought to be constitutive of desire and the sense of lack thought to be symptomatic of it, 26, 27; for an interesting critique of the notion of desire as infinite, see Goodheart.

desire and fulfillment—it is best to use this in-between state productively and strive for the beautiful and transcendent in one's work, even if fulfillment is ultimately impossible to achieve. Lapolla represents this ideal through the figure of the artist, in this case Giovanni Dantone, the illegitimate second-generation son of Agnese Filoppina and Padre Gelsomino, who finds himself caught between the desire of daily life in Italian Harlem and the fulfillment of an artistic dream he cannot quite name. This condition reiterates itself through a number of analogous binaries Giovanni negotiates through his art, which is productively located in the middle-ground between the mundane and the sublime, the bodily and the transcendent, the real and the romantic, and ultimately, between the Italian and the American. Neither side of these binaries is wholly achievable, and, in Lapolla's creative vision, this is for the best, for the artist operates best within the give and take of these polar opposites, using the everyday world as a starting point for art that ideally transcends any locality or temporality. Thus, for Lapolla, the Italian-American artist ideally would desire to create Italian-American art that uses *italianità* as a starting point for a conversation with a broader national, even international, community. As we shall see, Giovanni's artistic journey is a representation of Lapolla's own middle-ground between realism and romanticism and between his Italian past and his American future, for he used Italian subject matter as a starting point for fiction that ultimately resists easy ethnic or generic categorization.

The novel begins in late-nineteenth-century Villetto, Italy, where the well-liked Padre Gelsomino is performing the ceremony of Annunciation, only to be interrupted by a proud and defiant Agnese Filoppina, who rushes into the church clutching their illegitimate son Giovanni and, performing her own Annunciation, accuses the beloved priest in no uncertain terms: "Unholy villain, this is your child."[11] In the wake of the ensuing public scandal, Agnese, after refusing nearly every other eligible bachelor in the town, lovelessly marries Michele Dantone, "barber's apprentice" and "town stupid," and departs with him, her father Gesualdo, and her brother Luigi, for America. Gifted with aggressive, if not always ethical, business acumen, Agnese arranges while still on the "Conte Bertoldi" for *padrone* Francesco Crino to help open a barbershop for Michele, which touches off the business plot of the novel. Once in Italian Harlem, the Dantones become upwardly mobile due almost entirely to Agnese's shrewdness and acquistiveness, and they are able to move from a comparatively humble abode to a brownstone (*FITF* 98). While Luigi becomes a successful contractor, Agnese, never satisfied with what the Dantones already have, buys a share of the city dump and takes control of a number of junk shops, only later to enter into an agreement with Luigi and rival contractor Antonio Farinella to purchase property and build a row of houses (*FITF* 125). Simultaneous with the business plot is a complex love plot in which Agnese mutually desires not Michele, whom she does not love, but Padre Gelsomino and Antonio Farinella, her erstwhile business rival. Gelsomino, meanwhile, has left his parish and the priesthood—as if in an explicit attempt to evade the Foucauldian "pastoral authority," indeed the "law [...] constitutive of desire" that codifies "licit and illicit" sex—and travels to America in the hope of reuniting with Giovanni and Agnese.[12] Additionally, Lapolla crafts

---

11   Lapolla, *The Fire in the Flesh*, 5. Hereafter referred to in the text as "*FITF*."
12   Foucault, *The History of Sexuality, Volume II: The Use of Pleasure*, 92; Foucault, *The History of Sexuality, Volume I: An Introduction*, 83.

a family plot centered around Giovanni, a sensitive, young, artist and intellectual who does well in school but receives no encouragement, much less love, from his parents, who at best view him as impractical and idealistic and at worst view him as a painful and unwanted reminder of Padre Gelsomino and Agnese's adultery. Meanwhile, after her mother dies, Agnese exercises an iron grip on the family's affairs and reverses traditional gender expectations: "She dictated the family life, and her father and brother were glad to follow. She ruled unerringly and decisively" (*FITF* 8). Luigi and the generally emasculated Gesualdo and Michele are powerless to stop Agnese, for her acquisitive desires dictate every major decision the family makes. Indeed, as we shall see, desire lies at the heart of every major event in *The Fire in the Flesh* as if to exemplify Peter Brooks's later theory of "desire [. . .] as the motor force of plot."[13]

For example, the desire for familial love is a motivator for many of Giovanni's and Padre Gelsomino's actions. Giovanni longs for attention and affection from his mother, who does not understand his scholastic accomplishments and, with typical disdain for American educational institutions, believes school is "stupid" and "not for people like" the Dantones, who should go to work and earn money as soon as possible (*FITF* 29). Those familiar with the Dantones, fully "informed of [Giovanni's] origin," "had seen him grow up more or less looked after, but certainly not loved" — least of all by Michele, who hates him (*FITF* 44). Later in the novel, when Padre Gelsomino talks with his son, the two experience a mutual longing that Lapolla uses the language of desire — insatiable desire — to describe. As the two walk by the East River:

---

13 Brooks, 48.

Giovanni flushed perceptibly, he felt himself overwhelmed with a soft warmth that became a sweet pain in his heart. Gelsomino understood, and with the understanding came a pang of bitter longing that never turned sweet. [. . .]. The mood vanished almost the instant it was born, though it left the original longing from which it sprang even more definite and insistent, a yearning that was agony for the time when he could take the boy in his arms, and whisper the frantic secret, "My son, my son!" And Giovanni in his turn understood, too, and with his understanding came similar impulses, not aggressive ones, but a simple desire for the affection he had always lacked. (*FITF* 265-66)

In his depictions of desire, Lapolla is often careful to underscore its motivating power, its undefinability, and its ultimate insatiability. Giovanni thinks of his biological parents: "The slender hope of effecting some sort of union with the two persons who bound him at all to the active world was losing color and form, becoming the shadow of a substance. And coincident with it was growing a desire that was acquiring a force of will, and yet a will that could not dictate nor direct" (*FITF* 270).

Lapolla also lends violence—often retributive—great narrative power in *The Fire in the Flesh*. Giovanni's frustrated desire for familial love, particularly from his mother, manifests itself in Oedipal rage toward his father, who detests him: "There were times when the boy quivered with a savage desire to strike back, to kick, to bite," which he finally does (*FITF* 36). When Giovanni says that he wants only his uninterested mother to sign his exemplary report card, Michele gives Giovanni a "savage blow" the boy returns by throwing a stove-handle at his stepfather and running away (*FITF* 39). The desire for violence is also given ethnic specificity by Lapolla, who often attributes it to men desiring to preserve female honor. For example, Michele bites Antonio Farinella on board the Conte Bertoldi after he dances the tarantella suggestively with Agnese. Similarly, Luigi threatens Padre Gelsomino in the church scene at the beginning of the novel, and he later physically attacks Antonio Farinella for kissing Agnese after another suggestive dance of the tarantella at a party. By the latter portion of the novel, killing Padre Gelsomino becomes his monomaniacal obsession. Although Lapolla's figuring of Italian violence may strike contemporary readers as racist, it does demonstrate his willingness to allow desire—in many ways a product of culture and circumstance—to operate on a historical plane. At the very least, Lapolla is in this manner consistent with his predecessors and contemporaries, for, as Michele Birnbaum argues, "desire is always racialized and historicized" in late-nineteenth and early-twentieth-century American literature.[14]

Of course, the love plot of the novel is driven entirely by the erotic desires of Agnese, Padre Gelsomino, Antonio, and Michele. While all three desire the beautiful Agnese, she desires only Gelsomino and Antonio, leaving her husband perennially frustrated. In "Debate in the Dark: Love in Italian-American Fiction," Robert Viscusi argues that there is in this body of literature a "generational will that does not stop at the boundaries of the tribe," a tendency toward exogamy that manifests itself literally, thematically, and ideologically.[15] Indeed, erotic love functions as a metaphor of ethnic characters'—usually men's—desire to assimilate to American culture. The desire to possess another finds an easy figurative counterpart in the desire to possess the status and financial gain that comes with Americanization.[16] Agnese claims an

---

14 Birnbaum, 17.
15 Viscusi, "Debate in the Dark," 170.
16 Werner Sollors explores this idea in *Beyond Ethnicity: Consent and Descent in*

unusually large amount of power for herself in this literary tradition as a female character by being at least as much of a desirer as one who is desired.

Predictably, the business plot of the novel is driven by the desire for moneymaking, especially on the part of Agnese and Antonio. "Making America"—a motif that repeats several times throughout the course of the novel—conveys both the economic and social components of these characters' endeavors. To "make America" connotes to "make it" in America: to "make money" by America's rules and thereby be able to make a life for oneself. Agnese epitomizes this ideal of hard work and prosperity: more than every other character, "It was Agnese who sensed the potentials of wealth and exploited them mercilessly" (*FITF* 31). When she, Luigi, and Antonio move into the fields of contracting and real estate, they quite literally assist in the making of America, a point Lapolla hopes is not lost on his readers. American-style capitalism allows the immigrant the possibility for a level of success that was generally unachievable in Southern Italy. Thus, Agnese cannot understand Giovanni's lack of desire for money. She explains to Antonio, "Here I have been free to do what I pleased. I came with a bad name. But it's not a name here. It's what you can do. I wish my Giovanni would understand it. It means making money, piling it up. But they give you a chance . . . . They do not throw you out. . . . You are not damned" (*FITF* 114). This leads directly to the next connotation of "making America," which is making oneself American as one accumulates wealth. According to Agnese, in America, where they "give you a chance," what one is— one's "bad name," so to speak—does not mean as much as

---

American Culture, 160-66.

"what you can do" (*FITF* 114). The Dantones' first major step toward becoming American occurs when they move into a brownstone, which, according to Lapolla "had become a symbol in the eyes of the Italian and other immigrants to the south of the culture and wealth of the United States. To live in one was the ostentatious ambition of anyone among the newcomers who had achieved some material place in the community" (*FITF* 98). With the new house will come a whole new way of living; of course, the plan is Agnese's: "We are going to move. We have made enough money. Why should we live in this old house? I am going to buy a house on the block with the Americans, and we are going to live like them" (*FITF* 94). Antonio Farinella possesses a similar desire to make America, spurred in part by the success of the Dantones: "It had been evident that for some reason or another Antonio Farinella had been actuated by motives of jealousy in his feverish attempts to achieve a conspicuous, a startling success in America, a jealousy that centered in the desire to outshine the Dantones, if possible, and certainly to parade before Agnese each item of achievement" (*FITF* 113). Shortly after the Dantones move to the "English" section of Harlem, Farinella follows suit.

In the vernacular, "make America" carries sexual connotations that could not have been lost on Lapolla, as he clearly lends moneymaking an ineluctably carnal significance. In the novel, talk of money often leads directly to talk of sex. Immediately after Agnese and Antonio's above discussion on American social mobility, "Antonio got up from his chair, his olive features flushing with an embarrassment he could not control. There was a trouble implied in the nervous staccato sentences of Agnese which reddened her face, and communicated itself throughout the room as if a hidden force were dominating not only her, but him, too, and the very positions of the chairs and table, the unceasing ticking of the clock on the mantelpiece and the hissing of the gas flames in the colored globes" (*FITF* 115-16). Faces flushed, as if with sex, the talk of money leads to flirtation, which then leads to kissing (*FITF* 116). The "hidden force" is nothing short of desire itself, signaled by the novel's ever-present fire imagery and powerful enough to dictate everything from characters' courses of action to something as trivial as the "positions of the chairs and table" (*FITF* 115). Meanwhile, trapped in a loveless marriage analogous to that of Michele and Agnese, Catarina expresses her outrage at Antonio's lust for money and for Agnese. Her complaint moves quickly from money to sex, as if to underscore their common root in desire: "What do you care about your contracts? [. . .]. We got enough money. We have everything we want. We don't starve. More money, more money . . . . Why, why, why? She's [Agnese] got you by the neck, she leads you by the nose, she knows you're soft" (*FITF* 165). Then, the connection between money and sex reasserts itself in a dream of Agnese's that serves as an allegory for her acquisitiveness. In the dream, Agnese gathers sticks in a forest and uses them to clear her way but cannot gather flowers because of the burden they create for her—a symbolic indication that her moneymaking serves the undeniable practical purpose of allowing her to negotiate the forest of life in turn-of-the-century urban America, but it doesn't allow her to notice the beautiful in life as Giovanni does. As the dream turns to a nightmare, Agnese sees a grotesque giant hand reaching down for her and wakes to Michele groping her desirously under the fiery light of the religious cresset above their bed (*FITF* 190-92).

In the novel, characters also struggle with their desire for power. Agnese begins by taking power over her family, a decided reversal of traditional southern-Italian family structure that occurs, significantly, at just the moment Luigi is unable to resolve to exact masculine revenge against Padre Gelsomino: "The quickness with which she went about the task, the precision of each movement, the perfect assurance she displayed had finished the ruin of Gesualdo's authority over her, and implanted in him that dread of her words and actions which completely dominated him. And so, the actions of all of them were dictated by the unconscious submission to Agnese's imperious will which she contrived to exact from them by a pride and a self-confidence beyond their every-day experience to match" (*FITF* 20). Michele becomes a renowned member of the community due entirely to the efforts of Agnese, becoming a man sought after by Italian Harlem men for jobs and by politicians for advice (*FITF* 32-33). Michele cherishes this unearned power and his performance, for in reality, he is capable of exercising no power even at home, as Agnese is fully aware. She acerbically comments that Giovanni "ought to have had a father [. . .]. A woman it was I married" (*FITF* 46). Lapolla attributes this fluidity of gender to the relative freedom of America, in which anyone, at least theoretically, may lay claim to traditionally male power. This is a sore point for Michele, who thinks: "What a damnable country this was after all! Despite his timidities and his self-suppression he had never entirely subscribed to its code of conduct. It was not so much the male, he had perceived for many years, as the quality 'male' in man, woman, or child which commanded the respect he thought due only the obvious species" (*FITF* 123). With Agnese, Lapolla manages to avoid creating the "monsters of virtue or bitchery, symbols of the rejection or fear of sexuality" that Leslie Fiedler says are part and parcel of the dysfunctional treatment of romantic love in American literature.[17] He also manages to synthesize the "inviolate" man and "passionately desiring woman" that David Greven finds to be counterintuitively typical of male and female characterization in nineteenth-century American literature.[18] In her pursuit of men and money, Agnese is allowed to disrupt the desiring male/desired female binary Teresa de Lauretis locates at the core of Western narrative.[19] Furthermore, in her pursuit of men and in her use of them as laborers, she is allowed to disrupt the literary dynamic pointed up by Eve Kosofsky Sedgwick in which "the use of women as exchangeable [. . .] property" furthers the goal of "cementing the bonds of men with men."[20] In doing so, however, Agnese, while still identified and judged as a woman, must also shoulder normative burdens placed upon turn-of-the-century men. Thus, she is judged by both her ability "to regulate a moral or sexual economy" and her ability to negotiate a market economy.[21] So while *The Fire in the Flesh* can be justifiably considered as aesthetically reactionary in many ways, its development of Agnese resists such a summary judgement, for her claiming of "authority for the self both in the home and in the world," indeed her fusion of "both the narrative of history (located in the laboring and hungry body) and the narrative of desire (located in the sexual and maternal body)," brings the text markedly closer to the tradition of women's radical literature identified by Claudia Tate in turn-of-the-century African-American writing and

---

17 Fiedler, 24.
18 Greven, 29.
19 de Lauretis, 119.
20 Sedgwick, 25, 26.
21 Weyler, 3.

identified by Paul Rabinowitz in Depression-era American writing.[22]

Michele must resort to fantasy in order to console himself in his weakness: "He realized what he owed to Agnese, but he cried aloud to his own heart that she was as much obligated to him" (*FITF* 123). Of course, Michele here deludes himself, for in reality Agnese owes him nothing for their success, and Lapolla is very careful to reinforce his relative weakness. It is *Agnese* who makes the decision to begin the large building project: when Michele latently finds out about it, he can only "[stare] after her in the dumb way of a beaten animal" (*FITF* 127). After a party during which Antonio dances suggestively with Agnese and kisses her, "Michele stood behind the curtains looking out, devoid of the power to act, his whole body bent in an impotent huddle" (*FITF* 139). This weakness is disdained by other characters in the novel, for while Agnese is utterly contemptuous of Catarina's weakness, "despis[ing] her for" "the signs of fear in the timid woman," Antonio is analogously contemptuous of Michele's weakness (*FITF* 162, 163). When Agnese sells the barbershop in order to move into the brownstone, Michele is deprived of the one thing that had given him standing in the community, and he cannot bear that "they all despise me, ignore me" (*FITF* 190). When he reopens a barbershop near the end of the novel, he thinks, more than a little ridiculously, "Here *I* am the boss" (*FITF* 301). Lapolla is also careful to depict the power sought by Italian organized crime: the Dantones are occasionally haunted by the slick Paul Variglia, who attempts to extort protection money unsuccessfully out of Agnese, and then successfully out of Michele when he reopens his barbershop. Lapolla otherwise

---

22 Tate, 8; Rabinowitz, 96.

does not say much about organized crime but here gives mob power great narrative significance, for it brings about the climax of the novel.

Finally, characters desire the transcendent in *The Fire in the Flesh*, primarily in absolution for having sinned and in a quest for the sublime in art. Agnese seeks forgiveness for having "been strong-willed," for leading "one of the consecrated into sin," and for sinning herself (*FITF* 83). Later, she seeks forgiveness for leaving a window open in the room where Michele lay ill, praying that he survive. Gelsomino also seeks forgiveness for having sinned and for continuing to desire Agnese. However, this passive request for the intervention of the divine is given only limited power by Lapolla, and he depicts it as being somewhat disingenuous and empty—quite contrary to the descriptions of Italian-American religious devotion described later by Robert Anthony Orsi and Frances M. Malpezzi and William M. Clements.[23] While still in Villetto, Padre Gelsomino finds no relief in confessing his sin and directing his "thoughts" to "God" and the "Church." In fact, "The services he performed began to be empty gestures, blasphemous caricatures" devoid of any meaning (*FITF* 239). Similarly, Agnese's religiosity is called into question when she lights saints' cressets in the kitchen as "a routine gesture" and with "no more of religious exaltation or devotion expressed in it than in the movement of a middle-aged sacristan with his thoughts on the young widow he would give his middle finger to persuade" (*FITF* 96). Very significantly, when Agnese prays at Our Lady of Olivet for Michele to survive and that

---

23   Robert Anthony Orsi views folk religion as not only meaningful but also the single most important means for immigrants of Italian Harlem to make sense of life in the New World, *The Madonna of 115th Street*, 218; for a similar view of Italian-American folk supernaturalism, see Malpezzi and Clements, 113-32.

the Madonna signal his survival by keeping the cresset underneath the statue of the Virgin Mary lit until midnight, the opposite happens: Michele survives, but the cresset is extinguished by the church sacristan (*FITF* 287). It would seem that Lapolla prefers a more active approach to achieving the transcendent, and he represents this through the artist, Giovanni, who moves closer to God through his creative work. In fact, when Giovanni sees local artist Gino Birrichino paint, Lapolla has Padre Gelsomino tell him, "It's like God to be a painter" (*FITF* 110). I will take up Giovanni's art later and turn now to Lapolla's symbolic and aesthetic figuring of desire, which is essential to understanding the novel's title and creation of meaning.

As Lapolla suggests in *The Fire in the Flesh*, desire is an unquenchable, biological constant that allows characters to self-preserve but that also allows them the capability to destroy themselves. The power and ubiquity of desire is symbolized by recurring fire imagery that appears during scenes in which desire is foregrounded. The fire comes mostly from the gashouses of East Harlem, an eerie and imposing emblem of American enterprise, and from cressets in religious shrines encountered in homes and churches—a symbolic link to the religious desire of characters in the novel.

Fire imagery recurs in scenes in which violence is either threatened, contemplated, or enacted. For example, when young street toughs harass Giovanni after he has run away from home, "The gas house shot up its noisy yellow flare, and silhouetted the three gangsters against a background that was a line of distant roof tops and a foreground of broken, misshapen shadows" (*FITF* 70). This scene is one of many in which Lapolla uses Gothic firelight, and the consequent shadowplay, in order to represent desire's ability to distort perception and render the familiar strange. Giovanni is struck on the head while he is forced to participate in one of the street gang's dirty deeds, and he is returned home where he lies in a coma for an extended period of time. As he lies sick, Agnese admits to Michele that she wishes Giovanni dead, and at that very moment, "The kitchen windows lighted up with the red roar of the gashouse stacks" (*FITF* 79). Later in the novel, when Michele tells Catarina of his desire to murder Padre Gelsomino, his eyes are lit demonically by the gas light in his barbershop (*FITF* 311).

Lapolla also lights scenes of sexual desire with a persistent fire imagery. As Giovanni lies ill, Gelsomino, now a civilian, enters the room as Agnese prays to the Madonna for forgiveness. As Gelsomino and Agnese look at each other for the first time since leaving Italy, the priest's appearance is accentuated by the religious cressets of the room and turn him "into an over-dramatic chiaroscuro" (*FITF* 84). Later, when Michele tells Agnese that he suspects Gelsomino of having visited the house, Agnese's silence is followed by a "flare of the gashouse flame" that eerily alters the appearance of the kitchen (*FITF* 95). After the above encounter with Agnese, Gelsomino wanders Italian Harlem, which Lapolla lights with ample fire imagery: "the lights of the stores were like huge torches," and "the open cafés roared with flame" (*FITF* 258). Similarly, after their encounter, Agnese views avoiding Gelsomino as "a hypocritical denial of volcanic desires at the core of her emotions" (*FITF* 105). Antonio and Agnese's mutual desire is also signaled by fire imagery. During the aforementioned scene when the two discuss moneymaking, Antonio lustfully admires Agnese's body, which is fully lit by gaslight. When the two dance the tarantella at a party to celebrate the large building project, Lapolla describes the dance in terms of desire and again employs fire imagery to do so: "The elemental had burst through dams of routinized attitudes. Energy not meant to be harnessed had become loosed. Fire not meant to smoulder unused had softened iron sinews. The poppy seed of passion had burst into flaming petals which swayed to the music of tumbling waters and hot winds" (*FITF* 132).

Predictably, scenes of desire for the transcendent are also enhanced by fire imagery. For example, the scene in which Agnese prays next to the ill Giovanni is lit by a cresset under the Virgin Mary. Also, the scene in which Agnese and Gelsomino pray in the church for forgiveness — each initially unaware of the other's presence — the sanctuary is lit only by the fire of candles and religious cressets on either side of the altar. The importance of fire imagery in representing the persistence of desire is, of course, first announced by the title of the novel, which has not received the critical attention it deserves. When Lapolla figures desire as "the fire in the flesh," he accomplishes two things. First, he establishes the stubborn persistence of desire: the novel is, after all, unrelentingly saturated with fire imagery from beginning to end. Second, by placing desire within "the flesh," Lapolla roots it firmly within our biological natures. No one, whether they are as powerful as Agnese or as holy as Padre Gelsomino, is able to rid him or herself of desire. As we might expect, the title asserts itself, sometimes literally, in scenes of desire. When Gelsomino encounters Agnese praying in Giovanni's bedroom, he passionately holds her hand, and "[s]he made no struggle to withdraw her hand, to move away from him, to evade his gaze that was becoming steadier and steadier, a shaft of light from a burning lamp sheathed in charred flesh, that burned her as it had burned him" (*FITF* 85). Later, when Antonio expresses his love for Agnese, he figures this love as fire in the flesh: "Agnese, you are a fire in me. You have burned up my heart" (*FITF* 148). Later, his desire for Agnese is described as "an intermittent fire burning in his heart" and still later as "a hot flame in" him (*FITF* 166, 320). When Agnese apologizes to Catarina for seducing Antonio, she wonders, "How should I know what is in men that burns them with such stupid feelings?" (*FITF* 175). However, as Agnese is aware, the fire in the flesh is not specific to men. This desire can be read in the gaze of quite literally everyone, and it knows no satisfaction. When Antonio looks at Agnese, "he could see in her eyes the never-ending light constantly hinting of a passion that yearned but could never be stilled, of a force which challenged and denied, of a power which controlled and could not be moved" (*FITF* 116).

The supreme power of desire is given special significance in the text when the reader realizes that one desire is often linked causally with another. For example, Giovanni's frustrated desire for familial love leads directly to violence against his father. Analogously, Antonio's frustrated sexual desire for Agnese manifests itself in violence toward his wife (*FITF* 168-69). As we have already seen, sexual indiscretions often lead directly to retributive violence. The improvisatory sexual abandon of the tarantella dance leads directly to violence in two cases: Michele bites Antonio after the dance on the Conte Bertoldi, and later Luigi assaults Antonio after Antonio kisses Agnese during a dance of the tarantella. Also, Agnese's and Gelsomino's sexual desire for each other leads to desire for God's forgiveness on both their parts. The impression created is that humans live within a complex web of desire in which not only is desire never fulfilled, but also each desire leads directly, often unpredictably, to yet another desire. This point is driven home in another of the novel's allegorical scenes. After Giovanni befriends Gelsomino—not yet knowing the true identity of the man—Gelsomino tells him a story of his post-immigration travels in which two Chinese men gamble on a boat. When one man loses everything to the other, the other responds by murdering his opponent and robbing him of everything. Thus, the desire for moneymaking leads directly to the desire for violence. Agnese is disturbed by the story, perhaps in part because its depiction of acquisitiveness and its destructive end serves as a perfect allegory for the Dantones' experience in America. The significance is not lost on Gelsomino, who later declares, "What horrors of men and women are about us! They crawl all over each other. If they can, they sink their feet into you, coil like slime around you" (*FITF* 271).

The destructive power of desire is underscored by Lapolla's depictions of grotesques who have been utterly consumed by it. During his travels, Gelsomino encounters a horribly disfigured Portuguese man named Alexandro who "hated everything" and "blasphemed God": "He professed to despise anything remotely resembling a woman, and yet had been collection for years the lewdest cartoons and pictures, and photographs of himself and prostitutes in the most obscene poses . . .Money he professed to despise with an insane hatred. 'Money,' he said, 'is God's contraption to make men stink. So he could hack up their bodies and souls without conscience. Money is a dead soul rotting with worms, see. It's offal from saints' carrions . . . . A bitch in heat enough to draw the angels'" (*FITF* 241). However, Alexandro is merely describing the ruin desire has effected upon himself. Just as his self-proclaimed asexuality is a lie, so is his hatred of money: later in the scene, he attempts to steal Gelsomino's money and is stopped violently by another man. Then, during a stint as a miner in Pennsylvania, Gelsomino encounters another grotesque, the equally blasphemous Martha Malone, who keeps a boarding house with her brother Luke. When Gelsomino resists Martha's aggressive sexual advances, she seizes the scapular of St. Chyrsostom and destroys it piece by piece, taunting the horrified Gelsomino and calling him a "god-damn saint" (*FITF* 253). Even when her brother is shot dead, she is only capable of a "lustful leer" as she moves toward the messenger of the bad news (*FITF* 255).

Characters attempt to ward off desire by sublimating it through their work. Antonio and Agnese both employ this strategy—and unsuccessfully, for the consequent moneymaking simply produces a desire for still more moneymaking.[24] Indeed, moneymaking, while certainly necessary for survival, is quickly proven to be an empty endeavor when it becomes the sole reason for a character's existence. Early in the novel, Gesualdo asks Agnese, "You have made your pile [. . .]. But what has it got you? You have made more money than all my family since Adam put all together. You're no better off, you're no happier" (*FITF* 42). Agnese devotes herself exclusively to her work and does so in part to forget Gelsomino now that he has returned, but this effort to sublimate her desires, symbolized yet again by fire imagery, is futile:

> For a second on the night of Gelsomino's appearance she had wavered, had felt the force of the passion that had moved her in the beginning, that had, in fact, meant summit moments in her life, would have yielded herself gladly to embraces which, though enflaming, brought peace and slumber to unruly nerves, taut muscles, heaving thoughts. But years of struggle, of cautious devisings, of intricate contacts had developed the habit of wariness and she knew that the more substantial portion of her life was the wealth she had accumulated, the houses she owned, the standing she had among her fellows. (*FITF* 105)

---

24 Freud, *Civilization and Its Discontents*, 26-27.

Her "resistance" is "successful," but it is also, ultimately, "a hypocritical denial of volcanic desires at the core of her emotions" that does nothing to quell her desire for Gelsomino. This fact becomes clearer when even Agnese begins to question the significance of her endeavors, even the grand house-building project:

> The singular fact in Agnese's life had been that ever since her confronting Gelsomino in the church she had not once wept. She did not once weep now. But the impulse was present in her. For the object ahead of her, this building enterprise that seemed so important, appeared utterly foolish, almost without point. It was like a flash of understanding. What would she do with them when they were built, all these houses, one after one, red brick like a mountain wall? She had made America, they would say of her. But what was that? (FITF 179)

However, Agnese knows of no other way of coping with desire. Much later in the novel, as she expresses to Antonio her desire for Gelsomino, she says, "I am going to say good-bye to all this. Work from now on, only. Work—that's the American cure. Work—and Giovanni—work, Antonio, and nothing more" (*FITF* 322). Antonio has made a similar failed attempt to drown his desire for Agnese in business: "The years had not brought him the peace that comes in the wake of routine. More compelling than all other feelings was this residual passion which had no assuagement and which kept an intermittent fire burning in his heart" (*FITF* 166). Finally, Michele attempts to suppress his murderous rage in his new barbershop, but, regrettably, it "was not proving the soul-soothing escape that [he] had intended" (*FITF* 307). Having "sought the seclusion of his own trade," he is still continually reminded of his wife's love for other men (*FITF* 308).

Desire is not only a narrative element, though; it also manifests itself aesthetically in a stuttering syntax revealing characters' inability to describe, even give name to, their powerful desires. For example, when Antonio attempts to tell his wife about his feelings for Agnese, he is barely coherent:

> But my heart burned all these years . . . it burned to possess another . . . to hold her body till it should crack in my strength . . . I bore an insult for her . . . deep in my heart there's the scar of it . . . men know about it and I have said nothing . . . stuck to my trade . . . built up the business . . . reared a family . . . been a good husband . . . but the fire in me was hot . . . it kept up and up . . . and now . . . and now . . . Catarina. . . . You understand . . . you understand . . . you will say nothing . . . you will do nothing . . . you will not get on your knees before that saint . . . *Porca Maria del Carmine* . . . you do . . . you do it once . . . understand . . . *santissima.* . . . (FITF 167)

Here, Antonio attempts to describe his desire—using the fire metaphor yet again—and his attempt to sublimate it through his work and family. However, Lapolla's repeated use of ellipses represents both the blinding heat of desire and Antonio's struggle to verbalize its nature. Still, he manages to reference desire for sex, money, and religion before dissolving into blasphemy ("*porca Maria*") and then violence as he shakes his wife roughly. Similarly, Michele's desire for his wife and his jealousy produces a similarly ponderous monologue, this time conjoining sex, power, and violence:

> in the presence of everybody . . . you keep on making a fool of me . . .put horns on my head in the sight of the world [. . .] I'm going crazy. Do you hear, I'm going crazy . . . You will make me crazy . . . Do I want to do anything desperate . . . because I love you so much . . . ? You don't love me . . . I know . . . I was a fool . . . But I saved you from all those tongues . . . Why do you twist your mouth at me like that? I'm not nobody . . . I'm not nobody

... I'm not... you ignore me... you and that man I bit... why did you pull me off?" (FITF 182)

As Michele grows more crazed, his stuttering grows more severe, particularly in scenes in which he attempts to express an insuppressible desire of some sort. Near the end of the novel, as he contemplates murdering Gelsomino with a rabbit knife, he says:

> L... look... ing for that old r... r... rabbit... knife of m... mine [...]. Got a b... b... bone handle... c... curved like a... .a...a...new m... m... oon. I used to... to...s... skin rab ...b... bits with it in V... V... Villetto... H... hope I c... can find it...F... friend... going to b... bring me s... some rabbits. Hope... I d... don't... have to use it... hate to c... c... cut anything... now." (FITF 311)

Soon after this speech, Michele keeps repeating, "I don't want to... I don't want to... I don't want to," as if futilely attempting to negate the never-ending "I want to" of desire (FITF 312). The overall aesthetic effect is akin to Lee Clark Mitchell's description of literary naturalist style, in which characters' inability to possess a will of their own—or in this case an inability to satisfy desires forever burning away at them—results in a "stuttering syntax" often filled with repetitions (not unlike Michele's "I don't want to... I don't want to") that "depriv[e] both characters and readers of an otherwise comforting sense of autonomy."[25]

Predictably, desire strikes a fatal blow to those characters who struggle most unsuccessfully to manage it, and in one climactic scene desire reaches a logical, destructive conclusion. Later in the novel, when Padre Gelsomino hears of

---

25 Mitchell, xii, 20-21.

local organized criminals' intent to burn down the massive building project, he rushes to warn Agnese and arrives at the brownstone at the very same time Michele does, clutching a rabbit knife in a murderous daze. As the houses burn across the street, Michele fatally stabs Gelsomino, and Agnese grabs the knife from Michele and stabs him in return. Just then, "everything about her achieved a sudden illumination as if a light blazed and roared close at hand," and this fire casts a decidedly Gothic light upon the entire scene as nearly each of the novel's desires reappears (*FITF* 339). In addition to violence, the desire for power appears in Michele's inability — once again — to perform his masculine duty and avenge Agnese's loss of honor. The desire for sex appears in Agnese's and Gelsomino's final affectionate words to each other. Finally, the desire for money appears at the end of the scene when Antonio rushes in crying, "The houses, Agnese," and Agnese now realizes that the fire in the flesh has the capability of destroying everything it had helped to build (*FITF* 341). If we accept that Lapolla uses the house as a symbol of the immigrant's standing, then it would seem that he is sounding a warning that desire has the additional capability of compromising Italians' New World status. As we discover in the final chapter entitled "Christmas Day," Michele is not killed but, rather, is reduced to a "simpering" "half-wit child" still plagued by desire: in effect, he becomes the last of the novel's grotesques consumed by desire (*FITF* 344). According to the narrator,

> It was obvious that the murder had left nothing but a physical breakdown in its wake. The mind had driven into the flesh the memory that would have become an inferno of shrieks and sight of blood steaming and puddling at this feet,

> but some merciful dispensation of nature had transformed the agony of the spirit into the impotence of the flesh. And by some subtle freak of compensation, it was this very impotence that kept Michele a helpless disordered bundle and made it impossible for the hatred in his heart to break through, stiffen his disjointed fingers, give his body the momentum of his savage desire to seize her, choke her with slow, sure force and leave her like a fowl kicking in the dust. (*FITF* 345)

Reduced to this state, desire is no longer even a cognitive matter anymore but has collapsed back into precognitive need: Michele has no memory of the murder but still feels an uncontrollable urge to murder his wife, who now cares for him as a still unsatisfying penance for her sins and desires. Luigi aptly sums up the animalistic persistence of desire: "They're like animals in a trap . . . like animals in a trap, gnawing at each other, and they can't move, can't get their teeth out" (*FITF* 346). On Christmas morning, Agnese views the row of buildings, now nearly rebuilt after the fire: "'Ashes—ashes!' she said to herself, addressing them. 'You're built up almost, and who knows there was a fire in you? Like me. Who knows the fire in my flesh—burnt up, all burnt up" (*FITF* 346). This, of course, is a lie because in the novel's final scene—at Gelsomino's grave—Agnese admits that she continues to love Gelsomino (*FITF* 348-49). She tells Gelsomino of Michele's fire: "but it's all hate—all hate" (*FITF* 348). However, she also tells Gelsomino of Giovanni's desire: "He is very sad. A fire burns in him too. He is always painting. Do you know why? Because he loves, and you are with him when he paints . . . " (*FITF* 347). This is significant because despite Giovanni's sadness, he is still the most redeemable character in the novel and is arguably its hero.

Through Giovanni, Lapolla seems to be saying that given

desire's biological inevitability, it is best to direct it toward good by finding the transcendent in one's lifework, and Giovanni does this through his art, the ultimate sublimational endeavor according to Freud.[26] Unlike the novel's penitent sinners who passively expect God to come to them, Giovanni's art serves as a way of moving him closer to God. To be sure, Giovanni is like everybody else in that he is permanently suspended between desire and fulfillment. By the novel's end, he is still "sad" and can never find complete satisfaction. However, unlike everybody else, he uses the tension between the polar opposites of this in-between condition as an impetus for creative genius. In Giovanni's thoughts and deeds, the reader finds him permanently and productively located between the mundane and the sublime, the bodily and the transcendent, the real and the romantic, and the Italian and the American. In this regard, Giovanni is Lapolla's characterization of the ideal artist, for, like Lapolla, he takes the raw material of everyday life and uses it to transcend the everyday.

Giovanni is introduced to the reader as a quiet, sensitive, studious boy interested in literature and art and thoroughly alienated from his parents because of this (*FITF* 28). An excellent student during a time when few Italian immigrant children were said to be so, Giovanni has an outstanding command of English, "his unusual juxtapositions of words achieving at times a fantastic poetry" (*FITF* 29, 30). Giovanni's perceptions of his stark Harlem surroundings clearly place him in the permanent middle-ground between the mundane and the sublime, between the bodily and the transcendent. As he looks at the East River waterfront after having run away from home, his

---

26   Freud, *Civilization and Its Discontents*, 26-28.

look was more than a survey of the scene. It was a singing in his heart, the whirring of many pigeons, each a thought, or a picture that never showed the full-face canvas but only a side or a tilted angle view. The same softness and loss of strength came upon him as when he traced a laborious lighthouse in his notebook, or a tree meeting the full wind and yielding. His pictures were all out of books just as his strummed notes on the mandolin were all out of his head, and in both instances a denial of the present, an overthrow of the immediate, a construction of a delight that was, and could not be. (*FITF* 63)

Francesco Mulas writes that Italian-American novels show "an appreciation for the city's stark power and beauty" but mostly broker in "the horror of the American industrial nightmare."[27] However, Giovanni, and by extension Lapolla, have a very different perspective of the American metropolis. Capable of experiencing the sublime in even the most imposing of urban settings, Giovanni begins with the reality of the present, but his imagination and his art transport him elsewhere. And Lapolla describes this longing for the transcendent using the language of desire: "Along with the sensation of living in a world not the one around him, came an actual physical restlessness, the same feeling that made him behave as if he were a tight-rope walker stepping high above roaring waters. What could he do?" (*FITF* 63). The two above quoted passages directly invoke accepted notions of the sublime, the notion of "transcend[ing] the human" "in feeling and in speech," theorized most notably by Edmund Burke and Immanuel Kant, who view this experience as an awe-inspiring mix of terror and wonder piqued by nature and artistic representations of it.[28] Like many turn-of-the-century American naturalist writers, Lapolla successfully extends this percep-

---

27 Mulas, 69.
28 Weiskel, 3; Burke, 39, 51, 57; Kant, 476-512.

tive capacity to the urban setting of his fiction, in which the interplay of architectural, industrial, and natural imagery that Giovanni craves evokes an awful sense of the infinite intended to move the reader beyond the literal referents of the text.[29] The effect is resonant with Christophe Den Tandt's notion of the "urban sublime," through which "the literary metropolis is endowed not only with infinite scope but also with unfathomable depths" typical of "romantic nature poetry."[30] Thomas J. Ferraro notices a similar artistic dynamic in the work of Italian-American painter Joseph Stella, for whom the collision of rural southern Italian and modern urban American experiences produced a painterly ethos not unlike that described by Lapolla. Comparing Stella's sensibility to that of Ralph Waldo Emerson's "nineteenth-century post-Puritan [...] sublime," Ferraro writes,

> Like Emerson before him, Stella felt part and parcel of something beyond the individual self, supernature, but Stella's stimulus to the sublime was urban, not rural; machine driven, not nature borne; and people entailed, not isolated [. . .]. [T]he techno-industrial cityscape *panicked* Stella to *the wellspring of ecstasy*; he felt the deliciousness of terror recurrently, yet as if for the very first time; and what, metaphysically, the techno-industrial environment felt like to him was the pulsing together of deity *and* demon through the mind-body membrane into the soul.[31]

Lapolla's own sketch work and watercolors reveal a continual fascination with the urban sublime as created by juxtaposing the bleakness of urban industry with the still infinitude of water. Figure 1 shows a scene on the East River in New York not all that dissimilar to Giovanni's painting. Taken from a note-

---

29 Kant, 495, 498.
30 Den Tandt, 8, 55.
31 Ferraro, *Feeling Italian*, 33.

book filled with unpublished poems and sketches, many of which are urban-themed, the viewer sees the smokestacks of the background given subliminal serenity by their reflection in the tranquil waters of the East River. (See figures 2 through 5 for further pictoral examples of Lapolla's fascination with combining urban/industrial and water imagery.)[32] On the previous page of the notebook is an unpublished poem entitled "On the East River: Midnight," an urban pastoral of sorts that imports the sublimity of romantic nature poetry into the stark, realistic surroundings of New York City, performing the same juxtapositional feat as the sketch: "And thou,/ The gasstack belches, and there spread/ the purple curls of smoke, and there/ Where star sheen lay is what was when/ There seemed but night and all things dead!"[33] Ultimately, Giovanni can be taken as a stand-in for Lapolla's own artistic motivation.

There is nothing Giovanni can do to satisfy his desire completely, and Lapolla uses three narrative devices to symbolize Giovanni's permanent in-between state. First is to establish Giovanni as a Christ figure—part human, part divine—whose mixed parentage—parishioner and priest—is given its own Annunciation at the beginning of the narrative. Second, Lapolla has Giovanni run away from home only to wander aimlessly and find no satisfaction. Third, Lapolla has him return to a home that—with Agnese's initial (after his return, she attends to his needs more carefully) and Michele's continual emotional neglect of him—is not much of a home at all. The effect is to place Giovanni in a middle ground

---

[32] Garibaldi M. Lapolla, untitled pen sketch; Garibaldi M. Lapolla, untitled ink and pen drawing; Garibaldi M. Lapolla, untitled pencil sketch; Garibaldi M. Lapolla, untitled watercolor, box 7, folder 4; Garibaldi M. Lapolla, untitled watercolor, box 7, folder 5.

[33] Garibaldi M. Lapolla, untitled pen sketch; Garibaldi M. Lapolla, "On the East River: Midnight."

between the "here" of desire and the "there" of fulfillment. Similarly, Lapolla's characterization of Giovanni's parents signals the boy's "in-betweenness." Lapolla takes great pains to depict Giovanni's parents as polar opposites in many ways, his mother a literal-minded peasant and his father a spiritual, educated man who appreciates art. For example, Agnese has contempt for American schools, deeming them "stupid" and "not for people like us" (*FITF* 29). She wants Giovanni to leave school as soon as possible and go to work for the family business, but Giovanni has other ideas:

> Something vaguer than making money, something with rose in it and a mist that filigreed away from it in tantalizing spirals, a gleam of water with sunlight in it, impossible pictures that came out of a mysterious fund of memories without name and outline—these were in Giovanni's mind. Their full power never came upon him except at night as he lay in his windowless room, coaxing sleep, or when he sat back in his seat while the teacher droned and catechized. They became then a stinging sensation, an experience of being dead—dead to the world of barber shop and school and street warfare. But he knew a sweet relief. It was to be alone—drawing crude hills and water, houses and fleeing rails. He picked at the mandolin strings on a quiet evening in the darkness of the kitchen, with its stove still showing fire. The teachers, he knew, could be no help. And so Giovanni groped through a world that was in reality darkness. (*FITF* 34)

Agnese's no-nonsense world of moneymaking and business deals—her embrace of reality, and reality alone—is unsatisfying for Giovanni, who views this reality as "darkness" and who continually searches for the beautiful in his surroundings. In an atypical intrusion, the narrator asks at one point, "Why was it she had not known that in him would be love, understanding of life, something better than making America?" (*FITF* 180). During a scene in which Giovanni tells his mother about Gino Birrichino painting a storm—a painting whose sublimity moves him greatly—we discover that, once, as a child, Agnese had had a similar experience of the transcendent in art. As she had watched an old sculptor in Villetto carve Saint John's likeness, "she had felt a presence that had not been, a conjuring of a life from the infinite beyond to which everyone constantly alluded" (*FITF* 108-9). However, this sensibility is short lived, and ultimately, "For all her strength of mind, Agnese still retained the naïve literalness of the peasant face to face with a reality that is really mystery to him" (*FITF* 109). Shortly after in the scene, Giovanni quotes Gelsomino as saying, "It's like God to be a painter" (*FITF* 110). In this respect, Gelsomino is Agnese's polar opposite. Unlike Agnese, Gelsomino understands art and appreciates Giovanni's painting. Also unlike Agnese, who forever lives in the here and now, Gelsomino is a man of God, always mindful of a world beyond this one. Giovanni, then, is productively caught between the practical worldliness of his mother and the spiritual otherworldliness of his father, and this in-betweenness is taken to be a virtue, for it is characteristic of the artist who makes use of the everyday in his or her work and thereby approaches but never quite achieves the transcendent. Gino Birrichino, the artist who shares a room with Gelsomino and who teaches Giovanni, is described in these very terms: "Gino was one of those men who have not made and cannot make the necessary distinction between the reality of the present and the dreams that hover over it and around it. Why he persisted in painting nobody could tell, for he was perpetually and precipitously dangling over the brink of poverty that already had reduced his frame to pencil-thinness, but had not, at the same time, chilled the fire that burned within it" (*FITF* 234). Always suspended between the "here" of desire and the "there" of fulfillment, Gino spends his life painting due to the fire in his flesh, and he is no less happy for it.

Part and parcel of this artistic "in-betweenness" is the integration of Italian and American influences. Though often figured as polar opposites in Italian immigrant literature, the successful character of early Italian-American literature typically brings the two into some kind of synthetic harmony.[34] According to Lapolla's vision, the Italian-American artist is best equipped to do this and, furthermore, *ought* to do this. First-generation Agnese and Luigi are uncertain what to make of their Italian past. When Luigi insists, "I have the Italian in me yet. I'm not American," Agnese replies, "This is not Italy, and I'm less of an Italian now than ever," leaving identity a completely open question defined only by negative statements ("I'm not American" and "I'm not Italian") and guided by a strict either/or framework (one is either Italian or American). However, it takes an artist to see the beauty in the fusion of polar opposites. Gino, like Giovanni, sees the beauty of his urban American surroundings: "No beauty in this country?" he lectures Gelsomino. "Bah . . . it's only country louts that can't see it" — and here the reader should be thinking of Agnese and her ilk. However, Gino also encourages immigrants to remember their Italian past. Gelsomino begins giving Italian lessons in Gino's home, and Gino is only too happy to paint signs advertising this service, but when the response is anything but overwhelming, Gino can only conclude: "They have forgotten their fatherland [. . .]. The beautiful tongue of

---

34 In "The Re-Visioning of New York's Little Italies," Lawrence J. Oliver writes, "Lapolla emphasizes the resilient and amalgamative nature of Italian-American culture; and his immigrant characters, with rare exception, consent to assimilation. They do not, however, completely abandon their ancestral heritage in doing so; rather, they fuse old and new cultural elements," 14.

Dante! What do they know of beauty ... the simpletons ... the louts!" (*FITF* 260).

Giovanni comes to represent the epitome of Gino's, and we may rightfully assume, Lapolla's Italian-American aesthetic. While Lawrence J. Oliver nicely connects Giovanni's work to that of Bartolomé Esteban Murillo (based on Gelsomino's comparison), describing the work of the seventeenth-century Spanish artist as akin to Giovanni's in its "fusion of exalted vision and sensuous details" and "gentle and compassionate tone," I would like to draw attention to Lapolla's description of Giovanni's work itself — something that deserves more critical attention.[35] In his most closely described work in the novel, Giovanni paints a monk walking in Harlem backgrounded by the ever-present gas tanks and the East River. In this painting, Giovanni fuses each of the novel's artistic polar opposites: the earthiness of East Harlem with the otherworldliness of the monk; the realism of the background with the romanticism of the subject, who, "eyes absorbed, wide-open, gaze[s] into a nothingness that he explore[s] futilely for meaning"; and the Americanness of the background with the Italianness of the Catholic monk, who may very well be a thinly veiled rendering of Padre Gelsomino and who is himself trapped between the demands of sacred faith and profane desire (*FITF* 262). Furthermore, the painting serves as a moving depiction of the "in-betweenness" of desire. Never able to find the meaning he is looking for, "the monk presented a picture of intense hope and moving despair, affirmation and negation, bewilderment and understanding" (*FITF* 263). Gelsomino at first does not understand the painting's unique fusion of opposites, and when Giovanni attempts to explain it, he can only

---

35   Oliver, "'Beyond Ethnicity,'" 9.

resort to the stilted language of frustrated desire: "He's a poor monk . . . I don't know . . . I can do them . . . but see, behind them I have the river, too, and the dome see . . . ." (*FITF* 264). The desire to create art is yet another fire in the flesh that is never to be extinguished; however, Lapolla privileges this desire above all others in the novel. Even Agnese comes to see the value of it by the end of the story, when she tells Gelsomino, "A fire burns in him too. He is always painting. Do you know why? Because he loves, and you are with him when he paints" (*FITF* 347). Even the purest of possible desiring subjects, "the child and [. . .] the artist" as René Girard would have it, can never "dispense with a point of contact with the outside world" and is forever desirous of escape only to have "the treacherous magician — reality — [brush] against the fragile dream buildings and [reduce] them to dust."[36] For Lapolla, this is hardly a tragedy.

The painting of the monk can be viewed as metafictional, for its aesthetics neatly mirror Lapolla's own — not only in his approach to visual art, as we have already seen, but also in his approach to fiction writing. Like Giovanni, Lapolla embraces the fusion of the real and the romantic. Realism places great value in the miscellany and the activities of the everyday world, and *The Fire in the Flesh* is filled with painstakingly close descriptions specific to the everyday world of Italian Harlem. We encounter the following description of the East Harlem waterfront during Giovanni's time away from home:

> The city was constructing a pier at the dock. Piles of lumber, huge granite blocks, stacks of bricks formed natural sheltering places for the boys' clothes. They were there in hordes, chasing each other over the glass-strewn ground, in between discarded cartwheels, refuse heaps, jumping into the water like rats,

---

36 Girard, 29, 30, 28.

> throwing the timid in, ducking others, shouting—anything to be moving, making noise! Tugs puffed with confident strength as they pulled their tows of barges. In the near distance green-banked islands held aloft a huddle of red brick buildings. A white slow steamer moved by silently. In the far distance there was a silver-like shadow of sails, or the low-hanging trail of black smoke from a barely perceptible stack. (*FITF* 62-63)

The preceding passage does more than merely list items encountered during a typical day at the East Harlem waterfront. Additionally, it personifies many of these items, giving them active roles and thereby conferring value upon them: lumber, blocks, and bricks formed natural sheltering places; "tugs *puffed* with confident strength"; "green-banked islands *held aloft*"; "a white slow steamer *moved by silently*." In each case, appreciable value is given to the everyday world, and Lapolla uses this everyday world as the starting point for his art. However, unlike the realist, Lapolla does not view the everyday world as the sole means and ends of art. Immediately after this description, we are told "Giovanni's look was more than a survey of the scene"—the gaze of the realist—additionally, "It was a singing in his heart"—the perception of the romantic, who sees beyond the "immediate" to a transcendental "delight that was, and could not be" (*FITF* 63). To use Roman Jakobson's terminology, Lapolla's literary language shifts between the metonymy of self-referential, worldly realism and the metaphor of symbol-driven, otherworldly romanticism.[37] Or, if you prefer, Lapolla's prose negotiates the terrain between "the Real" and the capital-D "Desire" of the desiring subject, or, from an analogous perspective, between the staid signified and the "heterogeneous" signifier, shattered by de-

---

37 Jakobson, 77; See, 11.

sire itself.³⁸ The text simply refuses the stable, some would say repressively violent, constrictions of social realism and exists in those fertile, indeterminate middle grounds between the real and the romantic.³⁹

Upon Leonard Covello's request to use the book as a document for sociological research, Lapolla fired off a curt letter saying, "Well, it ain't no such beast. It is just a yarn that happens to have the Italians living in Harlem doing a lot of things which they should not do and some they cannot help doing, and I am afraid of no more sociological interest than the numerous flies and bugs that infest Little Italy."⁴⁰ In other words, Lapolla never intended for the novel to be taken as pure social realism. In terms of mood, he sets the novel in the familiar homes and streets of Italian Harlem, but his continual use of firelight casts an eerie glow upon everything that is more consonant with the romancer's aesthetic and sensibility. In "The Custom-House" of *The Scarlet Letter*, Hawthorne describes firelight as conducive to romance writing because it renders the familiar strange and sufficiently turns one's thoughts from the material to the spiritual.⁴¹ As if obeying Hawthorne's command, Lapolla repeats this very effect throughout the course of the entire novel. For example, when Gelsomino and Agnese first meet in America—a scene that recalls Reverend Dimmesdale and Hester Prynne's first encounter in the forest—Giovanni's room is lit by the Madonna's cresset, which changes Gelsomino's appearance from a "frank, open portraiture into an over-dramatic chiaroscuro" (*FITF* 84). Similarly, the inside of Our Lady of Olivet, lit en-

---

38 Jameson, 183-84; Kristeva, 116.
39 Bersani, *The Freudian Body*, 82; Bersani and Dutoit, 41.
40 Garibaldi M. Lapolla, Brooklyn, to Leonard Covello.
41 Hawthorne, 35.

tirely by candles and cressets, and haunted by stern statues and strange shadows, is described in intensely Gothic terms as Agnese and Gelsomino pray for forgiveness (*FITF* 281-94). *The Fire in the Flesh* neatly intertexts with two literary precedents—Hawthorne's *The Scarlet Letter* (1850), a standard for American romanticism, and William Dean Howells's *The Rise of Silas Lapham* (1885), which virtually defines the genre of American realism. Agnese is without doubt Lapolla's Italian-American version of Hester Prynne. Beautiful, confident, individualistic, and embattled, Agnese "b[ears] herself with such modesty and quietness in the general life of [Villetto] as to be taken for a model young woman"—all characteristics attributed to Hawthorne's famous heroine (*FITF* 9). Hated by the women of her small village, just as Hester is, Agnese responds to their jibes and insults with "insolence" and "silence" (*FITF* 13). Furthermore, the first appearance of Agnese has her defiantly clutching her baby, just like Hester. Unlike Hester, though, Agnese openly accuses her lover in front of the townspeople and eventually escapes their accusations. Gelsomino, with his sinful secret, is Lapolla's Dimmesdale, a connection solidified by the fact that the priest's services become "blasphemous caricatures" to him, just as they do for Dimmesdale. The pathetic, revenge-seeking Michele serves as Lapolla's Chillingworth. Finally, the sensitive young Giovanni feels a prescient affinity for his father and a hostility toward his stepfather, just like Pearl of *The Scarlet Letter*. Lapolla's use of the house as a symbol for the self-made man's (or, in this case, woman's) standing is a clear reference to Howells's *The Rise of Silas Lapham*, in which the protagonist's primary social ambition is to build an elaborate house in the rich section of Boston. Also like Howells, Lapolla uses the burning house for rhetorical purposes. Lawrence J. Oliver has suggested that

Lapolla's approach may indeed come closest to that of Frank Norris, who championed "romances of the commonplace" that sought out real surroundings without rendering them lifeless through transparent mimesis.[42] I will take up the topic of Lapolla's American literary predecessors in further detail in chapter 3.

Given the textual and intertextual evidence, it is very difficult to place Lapolla squarely within the realm of realism or romanticism, and this is precisely the author's point, for Lapolla believes the author exists best in the middle-ground between the very same opposites Giovanni is situated between. It bears mentioning that Lapolla is also situated in the middle-ground between "Italian" and "American." An Italian who wrote and taught in America, Lapolla never discarded Italian subject matter in his decidedly American novels. Although he would never fulfill his desire to become a successful writer, his work is living proof of his first novel's thesis — that the Italian-American artist's supreme desire ought to be to create art that begins with the materials of an Italian-American past and evolves toward something else. By extension, perhaps as an "unconscious discourse" of the text, it would seem that Lapolla anticipates a new American subjectivity that begins with the "consensus" of past ethnic and civic narratives and, through the vehicle of desire, evolves toward a creative "dissensus" that, in turn, leads somewhere else altogether.[43]

---

42   Oliver, "Beyond Ethnicity," 19.
43   Tate, *Psychoanalysis and Black Novels*, 12; Girgus, 20.

figure 1

figure 2

figure 3

figure 4

figure 5

The Cactus Blooms
Miss Rollins in Love *and Italian-American Pedagogical Literature*

As a teacher and school administrator for over forty years, Garibaldi M. Lapolla was well aware of the value of public education in the lives of all children, immigrant and native. Indeed, scenes concerning education find their way into each of Lapolla's three published novels, but it is only in the second, *Miss Rollins in Love* (1932), that education is developed into the shape and size of a central theme. This novel focuses upon the relationship between a devoted Latin teacher named Amy Rollins and an earnest Italian-American schoolchild named Donato Contini as both negotiate the realities of a sometimes effective, sometimes dysfunctional, early twentieth-century New York public school system. In order to understand *Miss Rollins in Love*, it is important to understand what was at stake for Italian-American schoolchildren in the early twentieth century—what public education had been like in the Italy had they left, what it was like in the urban America they arrived in, and how familial attitudes toward education may have affected their experience. In many ways, *Miss Rollins in Love* is like a literary case study of the ethnic student, which would later be explored with sociological precision in educator Leonard Covello's important study *The Social Background of the Italo-American School Child* (1967). The novel dramatizes the limits of the urban public school's ability to assist and nurture exceptional Italian-American students, considering the difficulties of both their family lives and their treatment in an all-too-imperfect school system. Given Lapolla's lifelong role as an educator, a novel like *Miss Rollins in Love*, which focuses primarily upon education, forces us to consider the role of the novelist as an educator, even if that novelist was skeptical of novels' ability to instruct the reader. *Miss Rollins in Love* can be viewed as part of a tradition of Italian-American non-fictional and fictional works on pedagogy that takes influence from the thought of John Dewey, that begins in earnest in 1917, and that continues until the present day.

Italian Americans and Education

After Italian unification had been completed in 1870, the Coppino Law of 1877 mandated elementary education for all Italian children until age nine. In theory, this meant that Italian children would undergo a few years of education in which they would learn the basics of literacy and computation and then leave school to work, only continuing with further schooling if the student intended to be a teacher, priest, doctor, or lawyer.[1] In practice, the law was not effective for many decades after its passage and was essentially unenforced in southern Italy.[2] Furthermore, in southern Italy, schools were often in poor repair, offered poor resources to children, and employed poorly paid teachers.[3] As a group, southern Italians were overwhelmingly illiterate, which was both the result of and the cause for their often contentious relationship with public schools. In 1871, six years before the Coppino Law,

---

1   Lopreato, 156; Rolle, *The American Italians*, 117; Bayor, 15.
2   Alba, 59, 247.
3   Foerster, 96; "America's Interest in the Education of Italian Children," 485; Banfield, 22; Rose, 31-32; Egelman, 193; Covello, *Social Background*, 243.

there was ninety percent illiteracy in southern Italy.[4] By 1900, the figure had declined only to seventy percent.[5] Furthermore, between 1889 and 1910, southern Italians had a higher illiteracy rate than any other European immigrant group to the United States.[6] Of course, none of this had anything to do with the native intelligence of southern Italians as was often supposed at the time. It only meant that a culture that had primarily created and shared wisdom orally was now by law required to attempt to achieve some measure of literacy, a realm of experience traditionally occupied by northern Italian religious, political, educational, and financial elites — people toward whom southern Italians had developed a great deal of suspicion. Southern Italians worried that the ideas presented and discussed in public schools would compete with the lessons learned in their closely guarded family and social lives.[7] In many cases, southern Italians openly resisted the compulsory education of their children, and the weak enforcement of the Coppino Law ensured some measure of success at this.[8]

Southern Italian children had been well equipped by their parents for life in rural, agricultural southern Italy, but Italian-American children found there was little in their family background to help them navigate the demands placed upon them by American public schools, where, throughout the late nineteenth and early twentieth centuries, they generally did not excel.[9] Italian immigrant parents brought a fair amount

---

[4] Egelman, 193.
[5] Gambino, 252.
[6] Mariano, 57. On southern Italian illiteracy, see also de Conde, 108; Covello, *Social Background*, 244; and Kessner 40.
[7] Rolle, *The American Italians*, 117; Alba, 59; Covello, *Social Background*, 243.
[8] Egelman, 193.
[9] Alba, 61; Rolle, *The American Italians*, 117; Mariano, 59-62; Covello, *Social Background*, 417-18; Kessner, 96.

of suspicion toward public schools with them to the United States, and this often created conflict with second-generation children who would often be told one thing at school and then come home to be told the opposite. This conflict occasionally manifested itself in behavioral problems that unfortunately contributed both to the poor accomplishments and the stereotyping of Italian-American schoolchildren.[10] At times, educators were not very well versed in the cultural upbringing of Italian-American students and how it may have affected their experience in schools.[11] During the early twentieth century, public schools were viewed as an engine of Americanization, helping to inculcate immigrant students with a sense of American patriotism and civic participation. However, some educators attempted to Americanize Italian students, again, without any concern for the heritage of these students.[12] Worse, some teachers and administrators were overtly hostile toward the cultural background of Italian-American students, leading to overtly discriminatory treatment, or, even among more sympathetic teachers, at least a prejudicial sense that only so much could be expected of such students.[13] While Italian-American educators plied their trade in the United States as early as the eighteenth century—the earliest known music teacher Giovanni Gualdo dying in Philadelphia in 1771, the earliest known language teacher James Puglia working shortly after the Revolutionary War, and the first Jesuit higher educators appearing as early as 1818—by as late as the early twentieth century, very few teachers were themselves Italian American, and thus few and far between

---

10 Covello, *Social Background*, 390.
11 Iorizzo and Mondello, 118; Gallo, *Old Bread*, 56.
12 Mangano, 178-79; Mangione and Morreale, 222.
13 Gallo, *Old Bread*, 61; Gallo, *Ethnic Alienation*, 154; Lopreato, 160.

was the teacher who could serve as a positive role model, or at least lend a knowledgeable and sympathetic ear to the concerns of the Italian-American student.[14] This situation would not change until the middle of the century.[15] In the meantime, Italian-American students generally would be held in very low regard. According to Patrick J. Gallo, "Italians were pictured as anti-intellectual. Thus, they were stereotyped as poor students. Moreover, they were portrayed as having very low aspirations for achievement."[16] These students encountered discrimination from teachers, administrators, and fellow students alike, and the results of ethnocentric aptitude tests served to justify such treatment.[17]

Italian-American immigrants understandably developed attitudes toward public education that would adversely affect their children's performance in school. During the late nineteenth and early twentieth centuries, Italian immigrants tended to keep their children in school only until the minimum required age, at which point children were expected to work for the upkeep of the family.[18] It was not uncommon for Italian parents to lie about their child's age or even encourage truancy.[19] At the turn of the century, approximately 10 percent of Italian children in New York managed to stay out

---

14 Schiavo, *Four Centuries*, 264-73; Lapomarda, 285; Schiavo, *Italian American History, Vol. II*, 136-44, 186-96; Schiavo, *Italian American History, Vol. I*, 197; Gallo, *Old Bread*, 57; La Sorte, 143; Mariano 63-64.
15 Pisani, 108.
16 Gallo, *Old Bread*, 58. See also Lopreato, 155.
17 Nelli, 148; Rose, 84-85; Gallo, *Old Bread*, 58-59.
18 Foerster, 395; de Conde, 109; Alba, 60; Gambino, 255; Lopreato, 155, 160; Pisani, 160; Nelli, 146; Rose, 87; Egelman, 194; Tricarico, 22; Covello, *Social Background*, 328; Kessner, 84; Bayor, 16.
19 Foerster, 109, 395; Gabaccia, 94; Mariano 58-59; Covello, *Social Background*, 391; Egelman, 196.

of school entirely.[20] For cultural, historical, and experiential reasons, public school was viewed by Italian immigrants as hostile to the interests of the family, which preferred to manage the education of children by itself as it had for centuries.[21] According to Richard Gambino, to be well educated or "[b]en educato meant [to be] raised with the core of one's personality woven of those values and attitudes, habits and skills that perpetuated l'ordine della famiglia [the family's rules], and thus one was attuned to the welfare of the family" — only the family, and not the schools, could make a child *ben educato*.[22] Schooling beyond the required minimum age, and especially college, was viewed as only for the well-to-do and not for the average Italian immigrant child.[23] The southern Italian proverbial dictum "Do not make your child better than you are" sounds selfish to modern ears, but it also spoke to a not unwarranted fear that education would create an ideological rift in Italian families.[24] Some Italian-American children, initially receptive to public schooling and the lessons it teaches, would adopt their parents' point of view as they aged, thereby extending the attitudes of their parents into another generation.[25] At first, many Italian immigrants had no intention of remaining in the United States and instead intended to return to Italy once they had earned enough money to better themselves in their native country. Eventually, Italians would come

---

20 Workers of the Federal Writers' Project, 114-15.
21 de Conde, 109; Gans, 68, 245; Gallo, *Old Bread*, 61; Lopreato, 155; Rolle, *The Italian Americans*, 135-36; Egelman, 194; Tricarico, 22; Covello, *Social Background*, 328; Kessner, 96; Bayor, 16.
22 Gambino, 247; bracketed text mine.
23 Nelli, 145; Egelman, 194; Glazer and Moynihan, 199; de Conde, 110.
24 Nelli, 146; Rolle, *The Italian Americans*, 134; Glazer and Moynihan, 199; Foerster, 396; Mangione and Morreale, 225; Egelman, 194-95; Gans, 129.
25 Covello, *Social Background*, 390.

to decide that they would rather remain in the United States. As this happened, their attitudes toward the usefulness of public education began to change.[26] In addition, the Servicemen's Readjustment Act of 1944, also known as the G.I. Bill, made the dream of a college education, and all the social and economic benefits this can confer upon a person, more real and accessible to Italian Americans.[27] A third generation of Italian Americans would become much more accepting of public schooling than its grandparents had been and would be rewarded with greater social mobility.[28] From the middle of the twentieth century on, Italian Americans could boast of great success in education—even as educators themselves.[29]

John Dewey

Another force that helped contribute toward the success of Italian-American schoolchildren was that of progressive education, which was touched off by John Dewey in the 1890s and practiced by many American educators and administrators throughout the years of heavy southern and eastern European immigration to the United States. While Italian-American educators numbered few in the early twentieth century, some of those who did exist embraced John Dewey's ideas and tried to use them in order to assist Italian-American schoolchildren. It is impossible to understand *Miss Rollins in Love* without at least a basic understanding of the thinking of John Dewey and of those American educators of Italian descent who followed in his footsteps, such as Angelo Patri, Leonard Covello, and, of course, Garibaldi M. Lapolla, whom

---

26   Egelman, 196.
27   Amfitheatrof, 312; Alba, 82.
28   Whyte, 105-6; Rolle, *The Immigrant Upraised*, 319.
29   Musmanno, 239-40, 242-43; Pisani, 95, 108.

Lawrence J. Oliver rightly argues "could not have escaped the influence of [. . .] John Dewey."[30]

Progressive educators believed that school was not merely a place to absorb information within a broad range of "subjects"; rather, it was a place whereby schoolchildren of all backgrounds learned to be participatory Americans. According to Italian language professor Antonio Mangano, writing in 1917, "Chief among the molding forces of Italian life in America is the public school. With all its limitations and shortcomings it is still the bulwark in American life. It is the only institution that can in a large way inculcate American ideals and principles in the minds of the rising generation of children of the foreign born. It should therefore be the aim of every true American to bring under its influence and teaching every child of foreign parentage."[31] However, progressive educators also cautioned against coercing children to forget the heritage of their parents. Mangano argues, "We should encourage Italians to remember the grandeur of their history, to preserve the best of their traditions, to feel that, as a race, they have great gifts to contribute to America and that, as individuals, they will strive to be worthy of their inheritance."[32] He cautions against a "superficial Americanization" that may cause children to be ashamed of their family, disrupt their home life, or even lead to juvenile delinquency.[33] Progressive educators believed that schools needed to adapt to the needs of students and move from a subject-driven disciplinarian approach to an approach that catered toward the needs and experiences of the students themselves. In a word, the school

---

30 Oliver, "Great Equalizer," 115.
31 Mangano, 140; see also Lord, 221-48, and Mangione and Morreale, 222.
32 Mangano, 178.
33 Ibid., 178-79.

needed to recognize that it existed for the sake of its students, not the other way around. Writing in 1921, sociologist John Horace Mariano recognized that public schools often seemed to exist only to promote "uniformity" and "mediocrity." Instead, "The individual must be kept free and allowed to expand and become 'individuated.'"[34]

Italian-American educators understood that implementing the pedagogical ideas of John Dewey—most thoroughly articulated in *Democracy and Education* (1916)—could combat these and other problems. Unlike traditional educators, who prioritized "book learning" over the lessons children learned from family and even encouraged students to pay attention only to the former, Dewey saw much value in "hands-on learning" and thought it contributed greatly toward human development. He also believed that the values and lessons learned in school need not compete with those learned at home.[35] He argues that "when schools depart from the educational conditions effective in the out-of-school environment, they necessarily substitute a bookish, a pseudo-intellectual spirit for a social spirit."[36] Students should not simply be told that they must learn; rather, students are served best when they are made to develop their own desire to learn.[37] Dewey also believed that education built up not only the individual student's intellect but also nurtured an active and benevolent interest in the workings of the social order that the student inhabited.[38] In order that this interest be genuine and not imposed externally, the student should be allowed to explore

---

34   Mariano, 294.
35   Dewey, 9, 22.
36   Ibid., 38.
37   Ibid., 53.
38   Ibid., 99.

independently, to "have a genuine situation of experience — that there be a continuous activity in which he is interested for his own sake; secondly, that a genuine problem develop within this situation as a stimulus to thought; third, that he possess the information and make the observations needed to deal with it; fourth, that suggested solutions occur to him which he shall be responsible for developing in an orderly way; fifth, that he have opportunity and occasion to test his ideas by application, to make their meaning clear and to discover for himself their validity."[39] A truly democratic society encourages, and benefits from, variation and individuality, not enforced custom, for "[a] society based upon custom will utilize individual variations only up to a limit of conformity with usage; uniformity is the chief ideal within each class." However, "[a] progressive society counts individual variations as precious since it finds in them the means of its own growth. Hence a democratic society must, in consistency with its ideal, allow for intellectual freedom and the play of diverse gifts and interests in its educational measures."[40] Such a conception of education and society had obvious appeal to early twentieth-century Italian-American educators, who were concerned that public schools sought to erase every "ethnic" influence from the minds of their students or at least foster a crippling sense of inferiority. Dewey was a cultural pluralist who believed that students from the full spectrum of American racial and ethnic groups had valuable lessons to teach each other and that these lessons had an edifying, and not weakening, effect on American culture. He also believed in the ability of any student, from any background, to achieve academic excellence. While he was not opposed to vocation-

---

39 Ibid., 163.
40 Ibid., 305.

al training, he disliked the tendency for some schools to divert students into vocational tracks when they had not had the chance to prove themselves worthy of other educational pursuits.[41] Italian-American educators knew from their own experience that many otherwise promising Italian-American students suffered from this very problem—sometimes because of their parents' expectations or suspicions about education, and sometimes because schools simply did not expect Italian students to excel in "academic" studies. Ultimately, to John Dewey, school should not be viewed as a vacuum—as a quiet, rarified place wholly separate from the outside world. Rather, it should be viewed as a microcosm of that very outside world—even to some degree a functioning part of it, a "community school." This is how students not only learn to live in the "real world" but also develop concern for how it might be made a better place. Ideally, for John Dewey, "the school becomes itself a form of social life, a miniature community and one in close interaction with other modes of associated experience beyond school walls. All education which develops power to share effectively in social life is moral. It forms a character which not only does the particular deed socially necessary but one which is interested in that continuous readjustment which is essential to growth. Interest in learning from all the contacts of life is the essential moral interest."[42] This "interest" is not merely the stuff of education at its best but also democracy at its best.

Angelo Patri

In the late nineteenth and early twentieth centuries, Dewey's ideas began to gain in popularity in American schools, but

---
41 Ibid., 319.
42 Ibid., 360.

these ideas in and of themselves may not have been enough to assist the Italian immigrant children entering urban American schools. As late as 1921, John Horace Mariano recognized that there was a need for teachers who were themselves of Italian descent. He writes, reflecting John Dewey's idea of the community school, "the one great deficiency with respect to providing an incentive necessary to raising the low percentage of pupils of Italian origin in the schools of [New York City] is the lack of teachers among their own kind. If there were a large well-knit and actively operating corps of public school teachers of Italian origin interested in visiting the homes and families of the great masses of Italian-speaking people in this city, the great stopping-off place between the public and the high school would cease to exist."[43] The first such educator was Angelo Patri (1876-1965), who in 1881 emigrated with his family from Salerno, Italy, to East Harlem, New York City. He earned a BA in 1897 and an MA in 1904 and taught public school from 1897 until 1908, when he became principal of Public School 4 in the Bronx. Generally accepted to be the first Italian-American school principal, he would later head Public School 45, also in the Bronx, from 1913 to 1944. The author of many books on childhood and education, Angelo Patri may have been best known to Americans for his "Children's Problems" column, which ran in newspapers nationwide.[44]

In his influential memoir, *A Schoolmaster of the Great City: A Progressive Educator's Pioneering Vision for Urban Schools* (1917), Patri reveals that he disliked school as a child, particularly the emphases upon rote memorization and strict, even cruel, discipline. Still, as a teacher, he attempted this very approach with his first New York public school students and

---

43 Mariano, 63-64; bracketed text mine.
44 Workers of the Federal Writers' Project, 121.

found that it didn't work very well.[45] He returned to school to pursue an MA at Teachers College, Columbia University, and absorb "new ideas and convictions," but he was unimpressed with most of what he encountered until he studied John Dewey under Frank McMurry, a progressive educational theorist.[46] The Dewey essay "Ethical Principles Underlying Education" (1897) was particularly influential to Patri, who would be convinced that "the whole system of marking and punishment and rewards was wrong. It was putting the child on the lowest plane possible. It was preventing him from working in response to an ideal."[47]

Once he became an administrator at P.S. 4, he attempted to improve classroom conditions that plagued both his own education as a child and his early attempts at teaching.[48] He worked to make classes smaller and to get to know students and teachers alike.[49] Like Dewey, Patri believed that the school existed for the students—not the opposite.[50] Rather than encourage traditional drill-and-discipline methodologies, Patri wanted teachers to value the student's own thought, growth, and individuality.[51] Toward this end, he encouraged the teaching of subject matters "that held emotional values" and allowed students to express themselves, such as "drawing, composition, music, nature, literature"—the sort of subject matter, incidentally, that inspires protagonist Donato Contini in *Miss Rollins in Love*.[52] Patri understood that

---

45 Patri 2, 4-7.
46 Ibid., 9.
47 Ibid., 22-23, 10.
48 Ibid., 21.
49 Ibid.
50 Ibid., 25.
51 Ibid., 28-29.
52 Ibid., 30.

such educational practice would meet the resistance of parents, who may "covet knowledge, book knowledge for their children" instead: "Rich and poor alike want their children done up in little packages, ready to show, ready to boast of. They fear freedom, they fear to let the child grow by himself. Because the parents want this sort of thing, the school is built to suit—a book school—one room like another, one seat like another, each child like his neighbor."[53]

Patri knew he would have to enlist the cooperation of parents if he were to convince them of the correctness of his approach, so he asked for their help in extracurricular activities and encouraged parent/teacher meetings where matters of concern for the school and committee could be discussed.[54] An advocate of Dewey's idea of the community school, Patri was instrumental in the creation of a "settlement house" for students, where they would be able to convene, hold club meetings, and recreate.[55] In service of Dewey's ideal, the community was encouraged to remain engaged in the education of the students, and the students were encouraged to work toward the betterment of the community.

Toward the end of *A Schoolmaster of the Great City*, Patri offers a number of recommendations that may as well have been spoken by John Dewey. Here he expresses faith in "the three R's," but only if they are reconciled "with the changing social needs" of the community and world and made palpably relevant to the students.[56] Patri encourages teachers not only to respect but also to foster an appreciation of the diversity of their students. "Do not go to books," advises Patri. "There

---

53   Ibid., 37.
54   Ibid., 54-55, 58, 64.
55   Ibid., 82.
56   Ibid., 127-28.

is more philosophy—big, broad, human philosophy—in the simple folklore of some of the poorest and most distressed people than there is in most of the books than you read."[57] Furthermore, rather than holding the traditional view that schools would Americanize the immigrant, Patri believed that the child, properly and humanely educated, would "Americanize America."[58]

Patri's work attracted the attention of world-renowned progressive educator Dr. Maria Montessori, who in 1915 visited P.S. 45 when Patri was its principal. She praised Patri's work and told him, "You are preparing children to meet the realities of life."[59] Like John Dewey and Angelo Patri, Montessori believed, as she told Patri, that "[t]he mere habit of obedience is not preparation for life in a democracy. . . . The safety of democracy depends on the intelligence and independence of the voters. Intelligence can be developed only by allowing young people to deal with actual life problems."[60] Throughout his almost fifty-year-long career, Patri established a model of progressive, multicultural education that would influence countless educators, Italian American and otherwise.

Leonard Covello

The most famous Italian-American educator who followed in the footsteps of John Dewey and Angelo Patri was Leonard Covello (1887-1982), who, after his father had spent some time alone in the United States, emigrated from Avigliano, Italy, to East Harlem with his family in 1906.[61] Like Angelo

---

57 Ibid., 132.
58 Ibid., 140.
59 Wallace, 55.
60 Ibid.
61 Brown, 149.

Patri, Covello disliked the dull memorization, the harsh punishments, the mindless rule-following, and the general boredom of public schools.[62] He also came to resent at a young age the absence of Italian from the public school foreign language curriculum and would come to believe that this fostered a sense of inferiority among Italian-American students.[63] He entered Columbia University in 1907, socializing with fellow student Garibaldi M. Lapolla and earning his B.A. in 1911.[64] In the fall of that same year, he would begin teaching Spanish and French at De Witt Clinton High School, where Garibaldi M. Lapolla would teach English.[65]

After some early frustration reminiscent of Patri's, in which Covello attempted to employ the same method of instruction he had loathed as a child, he became convinced of the need for a more progressive pedagogy, rejecting rote memorization, adjusting his lessons to the needs of students, and "allowing time for things to sink in, encouraging questions, and giving the student's mind a chance to work."[66] Like Patri, Covello believed that children should not be made to be ashamed of their heritage. Instead, he believed that the backgrounds of his many students should become part of the instruction itself.[67] Due to his efforts, Italian was added to the De Witt Clinton curriculum in 1922, and Covello supported extracurricular activities for Italian-American students, in particular *Il Circolo Italiano* ("The Italian Circle"), a club for Italian language and culture that began at De Witt Clinton and

---

62 Ibid.; Covello, *The Heart*, 12-13, 41.
63 Covello, *The Heart*, 43-44.
64 Ibid., 67-68; Brown, 150.
65 Brown, 150.
66 Covello, *The Heart*, 95.
67 Iorizzo and Mondello, 118.

would spread to other area schools.[68] He also resisted the "intelligence-test insanity" of De Witt Clinton and other schools, nothing their notorious cultural and economic biases.[69] Like John Dewey and Angelo Patri, Covello believed that his mission was more than merely informing his student body. "We wanted to educate for citizenship," he writes in his memoir *The Heart is the Teacher*, "to make active, responsible, voting Americans out of these people who did not have the means or the knowledge to go about it."[70] Vito Marcontonio, an exceptional student of Covello's who would later serve New York in the House of Representatives, is just one testament to the success of this education for citizenship.[71]

Another would be Covello's participation in a movement, which began in 1931, to bring a high school to East Harlem. Covello cites Italian-American education leaders Mario Cosenza, Anthony Pugliese, and Angelo Patri as having been instrumental in the process that would bring Benjamin Franklin High School to the underserved neighborhood. All three, along with Covello, were opposed to a vocational high school, which some predictably had proposed to serve the local student body. Instead, writes Covello, reflective of the ideas of Dewey and Patri, "What was in the back of my mind was a neighborhood school which would be the educational, civic, and social center of the community. We wanted to go beyond the traditional subject-centered and the current child-centered school to the community-centered school."[72] Covello would be appointed principal of the high school upon its opening

---

68   Brown, 150; Covello, *The Heart*, 109.
69   Covello, *The Heart*, 150.
70   Covello, *The Heart*, 155.
71   Covello, *The Heart*, 152-54.
72   Ibid., 181, 182.

in 1934. Scholars have described the school as "reflect[ive of] Covello's holistic educational philosophy," as a practical application of the ideas of John Dewey, and as part of a broader movement of American community schools that lasted from 1929 to 1942.[73] Scholars have also noted that through extracurricular activities, community outreach, and even some political activism, Covello was successful in making the school a functioning part of the East Harlem community.[74]

Like Patri, Covello believed that the cultural backgrounds of students must be considered in order to teach them properly—a dictum that he believed should extend to almost all aspects of education.[75] While he believed that schools, at their best, would assimilate ethnic students to American life, he also believed that students should never be made to forget their ancestral heritage—something that leads not only to shame but also behavioral and learning problems.[76] Like Dewey and Patri, he was a cultural pluralist who believed that students needed to develop an appreciation for the multiethnic fabric of their communities. However, as Carol Iannone has pointed out, Covello's cultural pluralism was not the "strong" variety that shoves students into impermeable human categories and hinders their attempts at mutual understanding but rather the sort that means to work toward a "harmonious American culture."[77] Covello also believed that ethnic students would be best served if there were more public school teachers of their own background to serve as an interpreter of both cul-

---

73 Brown, 150; Johanek and Puckett, 33-47.
74 Peebles, 210-11.
75 Covello, *Social Background*, 1, 419; Covello, *The Heart*, 172.
76 Covello, *Social Background*, 407; Iannone, 42.
77 Iannone, 43; Covello, *Social Background*, 412.

tures for students.[78] Ultimately, Covello's idealism matched that of Dewey and Patri. He believed that education bettered not only the individual but also all of society: in other words, "that the battle for a better world will be won or lost in our schools."[79] This battle requires teachers who are completely devoted to their profession, who seek to understand the specific circumstances of all their students, and who prioritize the social and intellectual growth of these students.

Garibaldi M. Lapolla

The documentary evidence indicates that Garibaldi M. Lapolla's views were consonant with those of Dewey, Patri, and Covello. While Lapolla was not as prolific a writer on educational theory as the other three, the published and unpublished record he has left behind demonstrates that as a teacher and administrator, and as the writer of *Miss Rollins in Love*, he was a staunch advocate of progressive pedagogy not only for Italian-American students but for all students. In an unpublished manuscript entitled "Principles of Modern Educational Procedures," Lapolla asserts many of his core beliefs about educating the schoolchildren of his day. In general, he believed that "[c]urriculum should be adapted to the child." Like Dewey, Lapolla believed that unlike the view of learning proffered by the "older school program," which can be viewed as limited and bookish, "[l]earning is a form of continuous experiencing" and must remain "creative," "development[al]," and "of purpose to the child." Also like Dewey, but drawing particularly on the work and ideas of Patri and Covello, Lapolla advocates not only understanding the student's

---

78   Covello, *Social Background*, 429.
79   Covello, *The Heart*, 275; See also Perrone, 66.

cultural background and interests, but building upon them in order to tailor-make an education for each individual child. Ideally, the teacher would be seen not as an autocratic "director" but rather as a "guide" in the child's growing self-discovery through "deep, enriched experiences," not mere "subject-matter curriculum." Lapolla in no uncertain terms echoes Dewey's idealism when he says, "The school is an agency not only for the perpetuation of the ideals and institutions of our democracy, but for social improvement as well."[80] Lapolla also states this pedagogical idealism in the unpublished document entitled "Are Our Public Schools So Bad?", in which he argues that as goes the school, so goes the nation: "The schools, as one of the most significant agencies making for desirable cohesion in our social order, must be free to carry out fully the essential intent of their program which fundamentally is the extension, intensification, and enrichment of our democratic heritage." Schools must work to support the "American faith in an informed electorate."[81] Lapolla's published textbooks also demonstrate his student-centered pedagogical idealism. In the foreword to *Better High School English through Tests and Drills* (1929), Lapolla emphasizes the individuality of students' errors and states that explanations in the textbook are kept short because "teachers should be left free to do their own teaching."[82] Rather than recommend a top-down, cookie-cutter approach to the teaching of grammar, Lapolla instead advocates for a method that democratizes the classroom and adjusts to students' individual error patterns, even employing research to determine the frequency of specific errors among students of the age group the textbook

---

[80] Garibaldi M. Lapolla, "Principles of Modern Educational Procedures."
[81] Garibaldi M. Lapolla, "Are Our Public Schools So Bad?"
[82] Garibaldi M. Lapolla, *Better High School English*, iii.

was intended to reach. Lapolla would continue this practice in *Required Grammar in the New York City Public Schools* (1937). In the preface, Lapolla insists upon the teaching of a grammar that responds to the needs and the practical situations of students. He writes, "The critics of grammar demanded that the application of grammar to composition and speech should take direct account of the errors observable in the daily English of the students. Students were not to be considered as future writers of learned treatises but as persons living in the present, *speaking* English for the most part, *writing* it only occasionally, but speaking and writing it for practical, everyday purposes."[83] Given Lapolla's documented commitment to progressive pedagogy in his writings on education, it is unsurprising that these same ideas would imbue his one novel that focuses primarily upon education.

Miss Rollins in Love

In a mostly negative assessment of the novel, a *New York Times* reviewer describes Garibaldi M. Lapolla's second effort as "a ponderous, heavily subjective account of the impulses and heart-action of an inhibited school teacher."[84] Olga Peragallo, writing in the 1940s, was more generous. She considered the novel "more subtly and finely drawn, less carnal and melodramatic" than *The Fire in the Flesh* and "written with a richness and a fine mastery of the English language."[85] The novel interweaves two plot threads, one in part documenting the challenges confronting the exceptional Italian-American student Donato Contini, and the other in part documenting

---

83   Garibaldi M. Lapolla, *Required Grammar*, iii.
84   "A Schoolmarm in Love," 21.
85   Peragallo, 140.

the challenges confronting the idealistic, Deweyan educator Amy Rollins. Although the story Lapolla tells is by no means conclusive, the novel suggests that while Donato Contini finds success as a puppeteer and sculptor, many, if not most exceptional students like him do not achieve such greatness. Instead, they are neglected by a traditional public school system that is ignorant of immigrant students' cultural situations and unconcerned with their specific needs. Furthermore, such a school system is shown to be in many ways hostile to the efforts of well-meaning teachers like Amy Rollins, who notice and wish to nurture the potential of Donato Contini and students like him. While *Miss Rollins in Love* suggests that success is rare given the long odds, it also suggests that the only hope for success lies in the progressive, culturally pluralistic pedagogy theorized by John Dewey and practiced by Angelo Patri, Leonard Covello, and Garibaldi M. Lapolla. The two plot threads join together in a romantic relationship between Donato and Amy that has symbolic implications for the relationship between teachers and students.

In the novel, Donato Contini, the son of Sicilian immigrants, his father a master puppeteer named Emanuele, is earnest and serious in his studies as a young boy, but lives in what we would now call an "at-risk" family environment. His parents are poor, and his brother Giulio is said to have been a gangster who had been sent to the electric chair for his participation in a botched robbery that had led to a fatality. The reader also learns that Donato's mother had died of a broken heart shortly after hearing the bad news. Both Donato and Giulio are said to have had little guidance from their father, who, for example, would often strike both boys no matter who had misbehaved. The lure of the street had been strong for both brothers. However, Donato had managed to escape

Giulio's fate by immersing himself in schoolwork and in the marionette theater. Lapolla makes certain the reader understands the many challenges facing Donato and real-world students of his ilk. After a powerful description of Giulio's crime, trial, imprisonment, and execution, the narrator states, "It was in this atmosphere that Donato grew up."[86] Indeed, Donato encounters many pressures faced by Italian-American students in the early years of heavy Italian immigration to the United States. For example, he wonders if he shouldn't leave high school early in order to help his father earn money. At one point in the novel, he is placed in a reformatory for a violent altercation in a speakeasy. Even though he is studious and successful at school, he faces outright bigotry from educators such as Mr. Sidon and Mr. Crabbing who don't believe Donato and immigrant students like him are worth the effort Amy Rollins puts into their education.

Described by Rose Basile Green as "the incarnation of the missionary zeal and sincerity of altruists who have helped immigrants to realize their own success," Amy Rollins sees the potential in even the most coarse and untutored students of her Latin classes and views teaching as a kind of "work that satisfied and blessed" (*MRIL* 41).[87] Like John Dewey, and almost as if she were following the advice of Angelo Patri and Leonard Covello, Amy Rollins believes her "main objective as a teacher" is to "enter into the life of the promising students in her classes, know about their families and their surroundings, become friends with them and eventually a force in their days" (*MRIL* 44). As Lawrence J. Oliver and Martino Marazzi have argued, Lapolla demonstrates that this idealism inevita-

---

86 Garibaldi M. Lapolla, *Miss Rollins in Love*, 123. Hereafter referred to in the text as "*MRIL*."
87 Green, 74.

bly competes with the reality of "large classes, burdensome clerical duties, a sense of complete division between teachers and pupils, and a general air of pessimism and cynicism about teaching and its results" (*MRIL* 191).[88] One day as she walks toward Donato's home, one of many acts of teacherly outreach she performs in the novel, she ponders her teaching of language and literature and the edifying effect it has upon poor immigrant children, who might otherwise fall victim to the circumstances of their daily lives but instead are allowed to "utter the music of their hearts above the confusion of the streets." "Such was Donato," Amy reflects, "and such might have been his brother, Giulio, could he have been saved" (*MRIL* 192).

While some of her colleagues are sympathetic—like, for example, Principal Polter, who is loathe to administer heavy-handed discipline, has a friendly relationship with teaching faculty, advocates "heart-to-heart pedagogy," and views ethnic students favorably—most are not (*MRIL* 100). For example, there is the authoritarian Mr. Aborn, who in trying to establish control of Amy's classroom, refers to Donato as "pretty bad stuff" (*MRIL* 55). Then there is Mr. Sidon, a teacher called on for "disciplinary cases too serious in character to be considered sporadic or negligible," who berates Donato and accuses him of being involved in "organized crime" (*MRIL* 58). When Donato inquires about establishing a sculpting club, Amy consults with an art teacher, who responds cynically: "It's an idea [. . .] but who'll give you one? Where's the money and where's the program committee to put it in? Talk to the principal? What's he care? Who cares about art?" (*MRIL* 106). Eventually, Amy comes to see her colleagues as

---

[88] Oliver, "Great Equalizer," 117-18; Marazzi, "King of Harlem," 200.

"leering effigies around her," "frustrated in part by the limited pay of their profession, in part by the narrow circle of contacts it allowed, in part by the poverty of their own vitality" (*MRIL* 197). Amy herself on occasion struggles with her own despair over the state of her profession and the cynicism this could foster.

The reader is led to understand that Amy's Deweyan pedagogical approach genuinely benefits Donato. As Lawrence J. Oliver argues, "Amy [. . .] instills in her pupil-paramour a love of classical poetry that refines his sensibilities and that leaves its mark on his mature art."[89] While Donato is Amy's student, she is supportive of his desire to form a sculpting club, much as Angelo Patri and Leonard Covello were supportive of their students' extracurricular interests. Throughout Donato's academic career, Amy frequently encourages him to stay in school. After Donato is forced out because of trouble with the law, Amy encourages him to return to his studies. When Donato takes a college summer art class, Amy is supportive of his idea to put on a marionette show there with his father. When Donato is released from the reformatory, she makes room in her rented household for him to live and provides him with materials and with the support needed for him to put on a successful art exhibit. After the exhibit, Donato tells Amy, "It's yours, Amy—it's all the poetry you taught me out of Virgil and Horace and Juvenal . . . it's all the poetry you gave me out of your own life" (*MRIL* 346). A further implication is that Amy's teaching of Latin literature, in keeping with Angelo Patri's and Leonard Covello's recommendations, has instilled some measure of pride in Donato for his distant ancestral past. As Lawrence J. Oliver has ar-

---

89   Oliver, "Beyond Ethnicity," 12.

gued, Donato becomes a well-adjusted, assimilated, yet still ethnic, artist, and the titles of his successful works support this claim: "*The Pioneer Grandmother, The Immigrants at Ellis Island, The Marionette Director*" (*MRIL* 368).[90] Donato is not unlike the memoirists studied in articles by Maria Parrino (Rosa Cavalleri, Bruna Pieracci, Grace Spinelli, and Clara Grillo) and Caroline Pari-Pfisterer (M. Bella Mirabella, Louise de Salvo, and Marianna de Marco Torgovnick) in that his education does not quash his sense of himself as Italian American but rather affords him a more confident understanding of what Italian American means.[91]

Lapolla places Amy's professional life on equal footing with her romantic life; indeed, as the plot evolves the latter becomes symbolic of the former. Lapolla has Amy reject a series of suitors, each of whom embodies qualities undesirable for a devoted Deweyan teacher such as Amy. Stephen Bennett, for example, wants Amy to quit work altogether and live a carefree life as his wife. Mr. Crabbing is miserly, petty, even bigoted, and lacks the generosity of spirit required of the progressive pedagogue. Mortimer, a man Amy meets while vacationing in Italy, is a New York schoolteacher himself, and he shares the cynicism of many of Amy's colleagues. Much as he intertwines, even conflates, the desire for money and the desire for love in *The Fire in the Flesh*, Lapolla merges Amy's desire to teach well with her desire for love. As the novel progresses, Amy develops romantic feelings for Donato. At one point, when Donato is no longer Amy's student, she reflects upon what she considers to be her failure as a teacher: "Somehow it had something to do with Stephen, with Crabbing, with Donato. If it could but bloom and be, it would do more

---

[90] Ibid., 16-19.
[91] Parrino, 72; Pari-Pfisterer, 19.

than merely display its flower, like one of the plants she was so carefully tending at home. It would radiate color, it would burst into flame, and the flame would be warmth and fulfillment. In its radiance, teaching would acquire a new meaning" (*MRIL* 249). On more than one occasion, Amy compares Donato to the Greek god Hermes. Compared to the great messenger of the gods, "Stephen and Crabbing and Mortimer now lacked bulk and form, were nothings in a distant world that had suddenly become shadow" (*MRIL* 283). The reader cannot help but reflect on the rejected suitors' failures as love interests and as Deweyan intellects.

Taken literally, the reader might disapprove of the love relationship between Donato and Amy, which is first signaled while Donato is still Amy's student but is fully realized while Donato lives with Amy after his stay in the reformatory. Taken symbolically, however, the relationship serves as a hyperbolic statement of the need for a more productive, symbiotic relationship between teacher and student and the need for the traditional boundary between the two to become more elastic. The fact that Donato does *not* return to school after his stay in the reformatory, in fact finds success without school, and the fact that Donato and Amy's relationship is not allowed to continue suggests that at the time of the novel's writing, the ideal, Deweyan relationship between teacher and student had not been achieved. However, at the novel's end and in a chapter entitled "The Cactus Blooms," the reader discovers that Amy Rollins has relocated to New Mexico, where she lives with her brother Philip, who has recovered from shellshock after his service in World War I, and Donato, Jr., a young son she vows never to tell Donato about. So while Lawrence J. Oliver is correct to suggest that Lapolla was highly skeptical of the ability of the public school system he knew to assist most immigrant children, and that the bright Italian-American schoolchildren of his fiction—Giovanni Dantone of *The Fire in the Flesh* and Donato Contini of *Miss Rollins in Love*—find success almost in spite of their studies—the presence of a Donato, Jr., at the end of *Miss Rollins in Love* indicates an optimism for the future, when a better realized relationship between teachers and students will work for the benefit of generations of schoolchildren to come.[92] But why does Lapolla insist upon bringing Amy Rollins to New Mexico? It is likely because these desert environs allow Lapolla the use of the cactus metaphor he announces in the title of the final chapter. In New Mexico, Amy becomes a successful cactus gardener, and the implication of this is that the best of teachers, like Amy, are able to nurture the social and intellectual capacities of their students even in the harshest of environments, like those faced by urban ethnic students such as Donato. They are able to get the cactus to bloom even with the laws of nature seemingly arrayed against them. Lapolla may have gotten the metaphor from Angelo Patri's *A Schoolmaster in the Great City*, in which the author tells the following story after the first act of a play given by the students of P.S. 4:

> 'My friends,' I said, 'I have brought you here to enlist your collective help in the work of the school. Acting together as a moral force in the neighborhood you are more vital to the education of the children than is the school. You remember the story of the cactus plant, how once upon a time, the cactus was a fine flourishing plant with luscious fruit. Then there came a change over that part of the earth where the cactus grew. The mountains heaved and the wind shifted. The valley that was once rich became barren and the plants died. They all died but the cactus plant, which, in answer to the new needs that the changing earth brought, toughened its skin and grew needles

---

92   Oliver, "Great Equalizer," 120-21.

all over its body. The winds came with their sandy blasts and the cactus plant withstood their attacks. It had become ugly, repellent, and the beasts of the field could not touch it. Thousands of years after, a man came by who took the cactus plant and put it in his garden. Here there were no hot sandy winds. There was moisture and soft breezes and wonderful soil to grow in. The cactus plant changed and became one more the thing it had been in the beginning, a fine plant with luscious fruit. So it is with your children. You are the soil and the wind and the light in which the child, your plant, grows. You are the environment, the compelling force which by its influence, can make the children fine children, or can make of them warped and twisted natures unfit to live with, unworthy to carry on the ideals of your souls. Even if we could take upon our shoulders all the responsibilities of the home and relieve you entirely it would not be good for you and for the children. The children need you. You cannot afford to have the teachers take over your responsibility. You must share the common burden. You must all work together to make the conditions of life under which the children are living such that they will grow up healthy, intelligent, sympathetic, of fine American citizenship.[93]

From the idea that schoolchildren need to be nurtured, to the idea that schools require full community involvement, to the idea that education prepares children not only for work but also for American citizenship, this passage conjoins many of the recurring themes and stated ideals of progressive pedagogical literature.

The Novelist as Progressive Educator

Given that Garibaldi M. Lapolla was a progressive educator and that his second novel is devoted in large part to depicting the benefits of Deweyan pedagogy, it is not unreasonable to attempt to understand the connection between pedagogy and novel writing as Lapolla might have understood it. We

---

93   Patri, 65-66.

know that Lapolla was suspicious of the novel's role as propaganda. The novel, in other words, should not tell us what to think or how to act. However, the reader of *Miss Rollins in Love* cannot help but notice that the one of the novel's central characters, Amy Rollins, teaches in a manner consonant with Lapolla's own pedagogical views. It is with these two contradictory ideas that we must attempt to determine what this lifelong teacher who has written a novel about teaching is attempting to do.

In 1965, Nigerian writer Chinua Achebe published an influential essay called "The Novelist as Teacher." In it he discusses readers' receptions to his immensely popular postcolonial novel *Things Fall Apart* (1958) and theorizes upon the role of the novelist in informing his or her reader. He argues, "The writer cannot expect to be excused from the task of re-education and regeneration that must be done. In fact he should march right in front." Furthermore, he asserts that the role of the author is to "teach my readers that their past—with all its imperfections—was not one long night of savagery from which the first Europeans acting on God's behalf delivered them. Perhaps what I write is applied art as distinct from pure. But who cares? Art is important but so is education of the kind I have in mind. And I don't see that the two need be mutually exclusive."[94] Since this essay, many critics have examined his effectiveness as a novelist/teacher. James Miller, for example, has argued that this task of reader education extends also to younger Nigerians through Achebe's children's literature.[95] However, P. D. Tripathi has argued that Achebe's pessimism makes him an ineffective educator.[96] Meanwhile,

---

94 Achebe, 105.
95 Miller, 8-9.
96 Tripathi, 106, 118-19.

Garibaldi M. Lapolla

David Whittaker argues that the lessons Achebe teaches in his novels are incomplete in that they do not represent the full spectrum of the society they purport to represent.[97] For our purposes, we know from Lapolla's dislike of 1930s proletarian literature that he did not consider didacticism to be the proper role of the novel. So if he is indeed a novelist/teacher, he is not the sort that Chinua Achebe and critics of his work imagine.

Some critics have located a drive toward pedagogy in the use of experimental literary form. For example, Alan Golding has argued that Ezra Pound's ongoing critique of American academia was a function of "his commitment to the principle of 'discovery' and 'newness.'" Supposedly, this avant-gardist pedagogy would go on to influence Charles Olson.[98] W. F. Garrett-Petts has argued that postmodern writers serve as pedagogues by underscoring the importance of interpretive positioning and power in the construction of meaning.[99] But obviously, Lapolla was no postmodernist, and he was uninterested in the "pyrotechnical coloring and devices" employed by the high modernists of his day.[100] So just what sort of novelist/teacher was he? As we know from his lecture notes, Lapolla seems to privilege a fusion of romanticism and realism in fiction writing, whereby passion and mysticism is allowed to blend freely with the workaday minutiae of daily life. We also know that Lapolla was loathe to adopt the second-person discourse of the romancer, or what we might also recognize as the lecture-driven method of the traditional pedagogue. While Lapolla does very occasionally present histor-

---

97 Whittaker, 107.
98 Golding, 87.
99 Garrett-Petts, 568-72.
100 Garibaldi M. Lapolla, "The American Novel."

ical information for the reader—for example the short history of immigration to Harlem at the beginning of *The Grand Gennaro*—he is usually dispassionate and undidactic in his representation of Italian-American life through its language, ritual, and mythology. If Lapolla is indeed a novelist/teacher, he is the sort that David Covin describes in his assessment of African-American poet Henry Dumas: someone who "uses words and structures and rhythms that evoke the character of our lives."[101] While Lapolla does not pretend to produce a sociological document when he writes novels, as his testy exchange with Leonard Covello on *The Fire in the Flesh* demonstrates, he undeniably crafts stories that mimic the experience of Italian Americans in early twentieth-century Harlem, stories that do not "preach" to readers but rather offer them a rich array of raw materials for the reader to construct meaning themselves. Lapolla is not so much offering his readers a guided tour of Italian Harlem—as a traditional pedagogue might—but rather a field research assignment of the sort that encourages the reader/learner to engage in the kind of practical, hands-on, experience-oriented learning favored by Deweyans.

If there is any connection to be made at all between Lapolla's novels and his cookbooks, it is in this very pedagogical approach. If ever there were a kind of text that encourages hands-on, Deweyan learning, it is the cookbook, and in both of Lapolla's published cookbooks, he plays the role of the Deweyan pedagogue, keeping his explanations short and practical, demystifying the subject matter and underscoring its relevance, and empowering the learner to teach him or herself. In *The Mushroom Cook Book*, for example, Lapolla briefly clears up myths about the safety and exoticism of mushrooms

---

101   Covin, 204.

and tells the reader, "I have tried to make a collection of recipes that are easy to follow, that offer very little trouble, that are altogether practical and at the same time are most presentable, and that, I trust, are even exciting."[102] In *Italian Food for the American Kitchen*, Lapolla writes, "This is a cook book that anyone can use. Rumors to the contrary, there is nothing mysterious about Italian cooking. There is no 'art' to it. Nor is Italian cooking so highly spiced and rich that it cannot be enjoyed by everyone."[103] He also tells the reader, "I have planned the book to be useful and so practical that novice and expert, man and woman, provider for a large family and cook for a small one, housewife and restaurant chef, will all find it an indispensable companion."[104] Unlike the traditional pedagogue, who might separate students into subcategories based upon their perceived innate aptitude for various tasks, Lapolla starts from the assumption that *anyone* can be taught to cook if guided properly in the attempt to do so.

Miss Rollins in Love—along with Lapolla's other works that focus upon, or at least reference in some way, pedagogical technique—is part of a long tradition of Italian-American works that reveal the long life of John Dewey's ideas. Beginning with Angelo Patri's memoirs in 1917, continuing with *Miss Rollins in Love* in 1932, and coming into maturity with Leonard Covello's *The Heart is the Teacher* (1958) and *The Social Background of the Italo-American School Child* (1967), these works make relevant the ideas of John Dewey to the experience of Italian Americans. This tradition would continue with *Miss Giardino* (1978), a novel about the struggles and the idealism of a San Francisco high school teacher named Anna Giardino

---

102 Garibaldi M. Lapolla, *The Mushroom Cook Book*, 19.
103 Garibaldi M. Lapolla, *Italian Food for the American Kitchen*, 1.
104 Ibid., 4.

coming to terms with the challenges presented by the new ethnic and racial mix of her mid-twentieth-century Mission District students. As Janet Zandy argues in the afterword of the 1997 reprint of the novel, like Amy Rollins, Anna Giardino possesses "a belief in education not merely as the means to improve material conditions (and that is necessary and should be named), but as a means to inquiry into what it means to be a human being in history and to have that humanity developed and cultivated."[105] Whether intentional or not, the garden conjured literally by the protagonist teacher's surname connects well with the gardening symbolism employed by both Patri and Lapolla. This tradition of pedagogical Italian-American literature continues with *God from Afar: Memoirs of a University Professor* (2000), by James Schiavone, in which the author draws Deweyan conclusions about education throughout a long career of teaching biology and reading in New York metropolitan area and Florida public schools and then in the City University of New York system. So long as there exist the Italian-American teachers that Angelo Patri and Leonard Covello once called for, so long as they concern themselves at least in part with the welfare of Italian-American students, and so long as some of them put pen to paper to tell about the lessons learned from it, there is no reason to believe this tradition will not continue.

---

[105] Zandy, 171.

Making America
Garibaldi M. Lapolla's The Grand Gennaro

Beginning during the late-nineteenth-century flood of Italian immigration to the United States, Lapolla's third and final published novel, *The Grand Gennaro*, tells the story of Gennaro Accuci, a Calabrian immigrant to Italian Harlem who rises from a small-time laborer to owner of a junk business, and then "minor dictator" of the local Italian-American community.[1] By pluck, luck, and unscrupulous business practices, Gennaro is able to "make America" and become "The Grand Gennaro," in effect an Italian-American "Great Gatsby." Modeling himself after the worst of the robber barons, Gennaro, who at the beginning of the narrative is a penniless laborer, violently wrests control of his friend Rocco Pagliamini's junk business. Gennaro's assimilative program of hypermasculine greed and brute force is ironically underscored by the series of women he beds (consensually or not), molests, or otherwise abuses — before and after he finally calls for his wife Rosaria and his children Domenico, Emilio, and Elena. The fortunes of the once *contadino* (peasant) Accuci family from Capomonte invite comparison to those of the Dauri and Monterano families, who were *galantuomini* (gentry) in Italy, the Dauris having been minor landowners from Villetto and the Monteranos full-blown aristocrats from Castello-a-Mare. When the three families move into an ostentatious brownstone Gennaro purchases called *Parterre*, the Accuci occupy the first floor, the

---

1   Green, 74.

Dauri the second, and the Monterani the third: an ironic, if archetypically New World, reversal of Old World status.[2] As Rosaria remains hopelessly Old World in her thought, ways, and appearance, Gennaro falls for a younger, more Americanized, second-generation Italian-American woman, Carmela Dauri, who, unlike Rosaria, exhibits all the benefits of an American education. Meanwhile, Rosaria, driven mad by her strange American environment, stung by Gennaro's infidelity, wounded by her eldest son's death in Cuba during the Spanish-American War, and unmoved by Gennaro's too-late attention to her, falls seriously ill. Her only hope of survival is thought to be a temporary return to Italy, but she dies returning aboard the ship, freeing Gennaro and Carmela to marry.

Toward the end of the narrative, Gennaro grows increasingly uneasy with his aggressive Americanism. Gennaro humanizes his business practices, and, remorseful for having robbed Rocco Pagliamini of a livelihood, makes his old friend the manager of the rag business. Gennaro also sees the fruition of a long-term project: the construction of Saint Elena, the Blessed, a Catholic church for local Italian Americans. Initially a monument of self-serving hubris, the church, in Gennaro's state of moral reformation, becomes a kind of penance. Rocco, however, never forgives Gennaro and even stirs up discontent among Gennaro's workers, who threaten to strike for better wages. When Gennaro manages to settle the labor dispute peacefully and beneficially for the workers, Rocco, enraged by another defeat by his former friend, murders Gennaro. Gennaro, like so many other European immigrant protagonists—Abraham Cahan's Yekl and David Levinsky, Guido d'Agostino's Emilio Gardella, and Samuel

---

2   Viscusi, *Buried Caesars*, 65.

Ornitz's Meyer Hirsch, to name just a few — is made to pay for his hyperassimilative indiscretion.

While Lapolla's first two novels earned mixed praise from *The New York Herald Tribune*, *The New York Times*, and *Gazzetta del Popolo*, neither was as well received as *The Grand Gennaro*, which earned the most effusive praise from reviewers when it was published in 1935.[3] While not unequivocal in his praise, Fred T. Marsh described the novel as "absorbing," "colorful," "sound," and "spirited" if not "outstanding."[4] Rose Feld considered the novel "stirring, tempestuous," and among the best to fictionalize Little Italy while she found Lapolla's writing "splendid" and "impress[ive]."[5] *Saturday Review of Literature* and *Boston Transcript* reviewers of the novel, like Fred Marsh, described the novel as "colorful," though the latter reviewer was more laudatory and noted *The Grand Gennaro*'s "marked development" over *The Fire in the Flesh*.[6] Jerre Mangione, writing in *The New Republic*, who would himself become an ethnic author of great importance in his own right, deemed Lapolla "one of the best" American writers of Italian descent, even though Italian Americans had "produced no outstanding writers of fiction and few novelists of any type." And, according to Mangione, while Lapolla "has a tendency to melodramatize his materials, to buy excitement at the cost of accuracy," he still "succeeds in creating Italo-Americans who are vivid and alive and probably a novelty to the average person who, not knowing them intimately, is likely to draw

---

3   Review of *The Fire in the Flesh*, BR4; Sampson, 16; Review of *Miss Rollins in Love*, BR7; Prezzolini, "Stati Uniti: autobiografia e romanzo."
4   Marsh, BR6.
5   Feld, 4.
6   Review of *The Grand Gennaro*, *Saturday Review of Literature*, 28, 30; review of *The Grand Gennaro*, Boston Transcript, 3.

his conclusions about them from the gangster movies."[7] In retrospect, Mangione considered *The Grand Gennaro* to be "the most successful of Lapolla's novels."[8] *The Grand Gennaro* also garnered positive critical attention overseas: his archival papers contain extracts of praise from twelve United Kingdom papers.[9] Since then, scholars of Italian-American literature have noted the novel's importance in the tradition: first Olga Peragallo in *Italian-American Authors and Their Contribution to American Literature* (1949) and Rose Basile Green in *The Italian-American Novel: A Document of the Interaction of Two Cultures* (1974), and then, from the 1980s through the present, critics such as Thomas J. Ferraro, Robert Viscusi, Martino Marazzi, Lawrence J. Oliver, Robert A. Orsi, Richard A. Meckel, Carol Bonomo Albright, Fred L. Gardaphé, and Neil Larry Shumsky. In a statement indicative of the critical consensus, Thomas J. Ferraro considers it to be one of the most "sadly forgotten" Italian-American novels.[10]

This is puzzling, for the novel fits comfortably within a strong tradition of European immigrant fiction from the 1890s through the 1930s dramatizing the collision of Old and New World cultures and the struggle to establish an identity that brings the two into a viable, if uneasy, equilibrium—neither destroying the other. Scholars have documented *The Grand Gennaro*'s function as an acculturation novel that fictionalizes the process by which an immigrant becomes American as it cautions against overly aggressive assimilation. For example, Richard Orsi considers the novel a lesson in "explicit

---

7 Mangione, Review of *The Grand Gennaro*, 313.
8 Mangione and Morreale, 365.
9 "Extracts from Reviews of *The Grand Gennaro*."
10 Ferraro, *Feeling Italian*, 240.

disregard for Italian values."[11] Carol Bonomo Albright points out the lack of Gennaro's "behavioral restrictions" and his neglect of "Italy's humanistic culture."[12] Also, Rose Basile Green's reading of the novel focuses upon its depiction of "The Early Impact" of Italian immigration upon the broader American scene and its positioning of Gennaro Accuci as an "ambitious immigrant" who "reaches for success at some dubious costs."[13] Among those dubious costs is Gennaro's friendship with Rocco Pagliamini. When Gennaro steals his friend's business, Rocco, aghast, marvels at how Gennaro has rapidly acculturated to the worst attributes of American capitalism: "The touch of gold in your hands has been too much. We peasants are not used to it. It does queer things to us — the good it makes mean, the mean it makes brutal."[14] Indeed, throughout the novel, Gennaro's wild assimilative drive is often figured in terms of violence and brutality. Gennaro's intellectual assimilation is evidenced by his Social Darwinism, the ideological fuel for Gilded Age excess and a recurring trope in ethnic acculturation narratives of the era: "You have got to be quick and shrewd and have no fear — that's all, and the strong man is bound to win" (*GG* 38).[15] Other characters attempt to check Gennaro's selfish behavior by reminding him of his Calabrian past. Most notable in this regard is the priest Don Anselmo, who attributes Gennaro to the "fundamental sociology" of "a small group, without the restraints of an or-

---

11 Orsi, *The Madonna of 115th Street*, 157.
12 Albright, "Literature," 343.
13 Green, 79. See also Meckel, 128; Oliver, "Beyond Ethnicity," 6-7; Gardaphé, *Italian Signs*, 184; Gardaphé, *Leaving Little Italy*, 6; and Albright, 343, to name a few.
14 Garibaldi M. Lapolla, *The Grand Gennaro*, 18. Hereafter referred to in the text as "*GG*."
15 See Richard Hofstadter's *Social Darwinism in American Thought*.

derly upper class with power and position" — as in the more democratic America — "follow[ing] the lowest, and not the highest, instincts" once some members of it "achieve a piece of wealth and command" (*GG* 139). Lapolla uses Don Anselmo to give voice to a concern among some Italian leaders that immigrants would abuse the new freedoms granted them in the United States. In 1917, Baptist minister Antonio Mangano cautioned against Gennaro Accuci's brand of "superficial Americanization," which, borne of a "zeal for too quick external Americanization [. . .] by many of our well-meaning but short-sighted volunteer workers," unwittingly causes "boys and girls" to reject "the moral restraints of their parents" and "the authority of the home."[16] To be sure, no discussion of this novel is complete *without* reference to its fictionalization of the Italian immigrant's acculturative process. However, while *The Grand Gennaro* shares many characteristics with *passing narratives*, including the protagonist's assimilative strategies, his professional success, and his adoption of American ideals, at no point does Gennaro attempt to blend *completely* into white middle-class culture. Although greatly acculturated to American ways, Gennaro's manner and appearance are still decidedly ethnic, and he never leaves the locale of Italian Harlem to seek his fortune in the American mainstream. Gennaro's difference is perhaps best symbolized by the tell-tale earrings he wears, which once belonged to his grandfather. Taking great pride in having become a success as an Italian immigrant, he boasts early in the narrative, "I made America single-handed, and wearing earrings. I'll keep on making America and wearing earrings" (*GG* 66). Thus, Gennaro conjoins his assimilation with his proud maintenance of visible ethnic difference — and does so proudly and defiantly. At his

---

16 Mangano, 178-9.

colossal funeral, one attendant quips that had Gennaro been able to witness the event, he would have proclaimed, "I made America" (*GG* 364).

"Making America," that curious and outlandish locution with many "subtle and all-absorbing demands" to use Robert Orsi's wording, states the novels theme early, recurs often, and motivates its every action henceforth.[17] Literally, the phrase refers to Gennaro's and, contextually, Italian immigrants' participation in the building of America's infrastructure.[18] Readings of Pietro di Donato's labor-centered tour-de-force *Christ in Concrete* (1939) often underscore this very point and the subsequent irony of the immigrants treatment as undesirable "foreigners."[19] In his rise from junk laborer to builder and proprietor, Gennaro is shown to "make America" as if from scratch. As Gennaro anticipates the arrival of his family from Calabria, he has his new house Italianized as if to trumpet the immigrant's ability to recreate America with a distinctly Italian presence, "*to make a new Italy* in America," as Robert Viscusi words it:

> Painters [. . .] worked night and day. When they were through the walls had become dazzling displays of Italian landscape. Stromboli on the ground floor puffed out lazy clouds of smoke into a sky that was too blue for credence. Aetna on the next floor belched black horror, but all down its sides and for miles about, running with quiet romantic leisure, highly colored hamlets made their way to a cerulean sea. And on the walls along the staircases the conical Vesuvius smoked incessantly while huge sombrero-like poplars began to sway in the wake of the clouds over the Bay of Naples.[20] (*GG* 91)

---

17   Orsi, *The Madonna of 115th Street*, 155.
18   Oliver, "The Re-Visioning of New York's Little Italies," 15.
19   Ferraro, *Feeling Italian*, 52.
20   Viscusi, "Making Italy Little," 61.

As the church is built, Gennaro surveys the superstructure and tells Carmela, "Real American stuff [...]. Steel beams ... not your old wooden frames ... this is a building, I tell you" (GG 281). Lapolla is careful to exemplify "making America" in the most concrete terms possible.

Nearly all reviewers and critics of the novel point out its centrality of "making America" to *The Grand Gennaro* and how, for Gennaro Accuci, it becomes not only a *ragione di essere* but a monomaniacal obsession to be pursued at any ethical cost. However, a more thorough examination of the phrase's figurative possibilities is necessary to appreciate fully the richness of *The Grand Gennaro*. Rose Feld first acknowledged the plurality of meaning embedded in the expression: "'Making America' is an Italian expression which holds both the elements of contempt and admiration and, as the tale of this lusty, laughing, ruthless, brutal character gathers momentum in the pages of Garibaldi Lapolla's novel [. . .], one understands the many sided implications of the term."[21] Some sixty years later, Robert Viscusi explored its Italian origins, which, due to the double meaning of the verb *fare*, provide insight into the phrase's figurative possibilities: "*Fare l'America*. Make America. Do America. This phrase [. . .] names the enterprise of many an emigrant from Italy. *Fare l'America* means not only *to go elsewhere than in Italy*."[22] Figuratively, the phrase means "making it" in America or "making good," as the narrator offers as an admittedly inadequate "approximation" (GG 4). In the novel, "making America" involves all the characteristics of a male-centered American success story and bears special significance for the lowly immigrant:

---

21 Feld, 4.
22 Viscusi, "Making Italy Little," 61.

it means that a nobody, a mere clodhopper, a good-for-nothing on the other side, had contrived by hook or crook in this new, strange country, with its queer ways and its lack of distinctions, to amass enough money to strut about and proclaim himself the equal of those who had been his superiors in the old country. And if one said of himself that he had made America, he said it with an air of rough boasting, implying "I told you so" or "Look at me." Although [Gennaro] knew that his spectators would be inclined to despise him for the word, he threw out his chest. And yet there were comfort and solidity, the double fruit of egotism, in its use, and he used it, even roared it out, and laughed. Gennaro Accuci had made America, and he was not the type to soft-pedal the expression. He pounded his sturdy small chest with his rough-knuckled small hand [. . .] and declared mightily [. . .], "I, I made America, and made it quick." (GG 4-5)

However, Gennaro intends to sidestep all the Franklinian grunt work involved in the myth of success. When Rocco Pagliamini first hires Gennaro as a laborer in his junk business, he tells his friend with the knowing sincerity of someone who has done it himself, "You got to sweat, my son; you got to starve; you got to turn your own relatives away starving. For instance, will you take off your coat now and pitch in among these filthy, dusty, worm-eaten rags and let the dirt get mixed up with your spittle and your sweat and laugh anyhow?" Gennaro boastfully asserts, "I'm going to make America, and make it quick" (GG 8, 9). And make it quick he does. Gennaro quickly recognizes the reality of Rocco's narrative of labor and comes to resent it: "This was a dog's life, working for Rocco, working for anybody, fumbling through old rags, cutting one's fingers on tin and scraps of iron. What could he do on a dollar a day? He ate twenty cents of it and saved the eighty. What was that? That wouldn't make America. So he watched the boys coming in with old copper bottoms and pieces of lead-pipe. He took one aside, a slinking, thin lad with slit-like eyes that always looked frightened. 'One cent more a pound for the copper—half of the copper; the other half, the old price. But don't tell nobody'" (*GG* 10). Before long, through physical prowess and sheer cunning, Gennaro demands half and then all of Rocco's business before unethically conquering the local "old-rag-and-metal industry" (*GG* 17). "The King of Harlem," to use Martino Marazzi's descriptive, Gennaro's many parades, celebrations, and ultimately, the construction for the Italian community of the Church of Saint Elena the Blessed, the pinnacle of his achievement, intratextually refer to his success in making America, as do the other concrete images of his industry.[23] Even the aftermath of his murder at the hands of Rocco, who shoves Gennaro's lifeless corpse into a bale he then raises with a crane and swings over the East River, becomes a "blood-soaked symbol of Gennaro's success and failure in making America."[24] Supplied with a healthy dose of Dantean poetic justice, the scene connects Gennaro's punishment with his sin and renders him as solitary as his reckless individualism has ultimately left him.

Another figurative connotation is the assimilative impulse foregrounded in all ethnic literature. As Robert Viscusi points out, "To make America means to construct oneself," and indeed another meaning of the phrase that suggests itself, keeping in mind *fare*'s semantic double-duty, is the immigrant's imperative to *make* him or herself American and *do* as the Americans do.[25] *The Grand Gennaro* abundantly records its protagonist's insatiable hunger to act American, consume all things American, indeed, to *become* American so that when he

---

23 Viscusi, *Buried Caesars*, 148.
24 Meckel, 137.
25 Viscusi, "Making Italy Little," 61.

says he has "made America," he is clearly describing not only what he has done but also who he is. Upon losing sole control of his junk business, Rocco can only observe as he signs over half of his enterprise, "Well, you have made America, and made it quick. You were born an American" (GG 12). When he is forced out completely, he accuses Gennaro of having "the American fever," a tendency among upwardly mobile immigrants unaccustomed to wealth and prestige to embody the most destructive attributes of capitalism (GG 18). In the fictional world of *The Grand Gennaro*, becoming American necessitates cultivating a lust for moneymaking. When Gennaro helps create a new millinery business for Davido Monterano, the dandified don exclaims, more than a little ridiculously,

> Ah, my marvelous Gennaro, you create energy within me, great and glowing flames of life, as if my whole being is being remade in the furnace of American ideals. And it is, sir, it is. You have known how to subdue the inclement winds of adversity to your own purposes. That, I take it, is the American ideal, pinnacle of modern thinking. [. . .] Take this store we are jointly creating. What a thought! The essence of business acumen! It moves the stars, Gennaro, and all the other worlds, for it is greater than all things, business ability, greater than even love. (GG 226)

However, Davido Monterano is at best a figurehead of a business owner who contributes little to the day-to-day affairs of the millinery center and, foiled by Gennaro in his pursuit of Carmela Dauri and mystified by his New World subservience to the former *contadino*, he "collapse[s] into a self-pitying, helpless old man sustained only by his passionate adherence to Old World conceptions of greatness" (GG 259). When he dies crazed and destitute, Gennaro knows exactly why: "He could never be an American. He could never make America. His life was in Italy, and to that could he go back?" (*GG* 277). None of this is to suggest that Gennaro's success comes entirely at the cost of his Italian past. Immigrant texts often privilege a deft negotiation of Old and New World influences—a state of being in which Gennaro's earrings may appear "bright and shining" "not" as "incongruous ornaments" of the Old World worn by a man with New World aspirations but truly "part of the man"—that ruptures the traditional dichotomization of the two (*GG* 239).[26] As Thomas Ferraro has demonstrated in his readings of Anzia Yezeierska's *Bread Givers* (1925) and Mario Puzo's *The Godfather* (1969), American immigrant literature often puts Old World folkways in the very service of accruing New World wealth.[27] Gennaro continues to identify as a once lowly Calabrian immigrant, and his "unabashed and unembarrassed" wearing of his father's earrings, "the signs of [his] origins"; his many ethnic festivals and festivals; his service to his fellow Italian immigrants; his establishment of an Italian millinery business; and his construction of an Italian church—all serve to further his wealth and prestige and all necessarily assist in Gennaro's self-fashioning as an American, his making himself American and doing as the Americans do (*GG* 226).

Gennaro's socioeconomic transformation into an American, his Columbian "discovery" and "conquest" of America, has a symbolic analogue in the series of women he attempts to claim as the spoils of his imperial victory. Indeed, the suggestive phrase "making America" cleverly conjoins Gennaro's assimilative drive with its sexual underbelly, and Lapolla is careful to lend cultural valence to the protagonist's

---

26 Orsi, "The Fault of Memory," 138.
27 See chapters 1 and 2 of Thomas Ferraro, *Ethnic Passages: Literary Immigrants in Twentieth-Century America*.

victims and love interests. In doing so, Lapolla is extending a historiographic trope that has long captivated Americans, for it is not without precedent to represent the European subjugation of North America in frankly sexual terms. As Henry Nash Smith argues in his evocatively titled classic *Virgin Land: The American West as Symbol and Myth* (1950), "one of the most persistent generalizations concerning American life and character is the notion that our society has been shaped by the pull of a vacant continent drawing population westward through the passes of the Alleghenies, across the Mississippi Valley, over the high plains and mountains of the Far West to the Pacific Coast."[28] Smith argues that, after independence was won, this sense of "continental destiny" predominated the way America viewed itself.[29] "Conquest" of the continent would come to create "the historical bedrock of the whole nation."[30] As Fred T. Marsh was the first to point out, American conquest certainly forms the basis of Gennaro's claims to "making America," as he follows the transatlantic path of his discoverer forbears and lays claim to everything he sees.[31] Additionally, in the imagination of European Americans of the Early Republic, the unsettled wilderness "is presented as a new and enchanting region of inexpressible beauty and fertility"—feminine qualities beckoning the male conqueror.[32] Thus, the exploration and settling of the continent, indeed, "the conquest of America," as Tzvetan Todorov describes it in his historical and theoretical study of the same name, seems almost inevitably to coincide with

---

28 Smith, 3.
29 Ibid., 9.
30 Limerick, 27.
31 Marsh, "The Grand Gennaro," BR6.
32 Smith, *Virgin Land*, 11.

the subjugation and exploitation of its native women.[33] The female American continent awaits, indeed requires, the rule of the male conqueror. The literary symbolism of this mythology is perhaps best explored by Annette Kolodny in *The Lay of the Land* (1975), in which she argues, "America's oldest and most cherished fantasy" is "a daily reality of harmony between man and nature based on the experience of the land as essentially feminine [. . .] enclosing the individual in an environment of receptivity, repose, and painless and integral satisfaction."[34] Additionally, "Eden, Paradise, the Golden Age, and the idyllic garden, in short, all the backdrops for European literary pastoral, were subsumed in the image of an America promising material ease without labor or hardship, as opposed to the grinding poverty of previous European existence."[35] Under the sway of this mythology, John Rolfe's 1614 marriage to Pocahontas would take on enormous symbolic significance, and America's entire literary tradition, from its pastoral beginnings — in which the New World significantly was personified as "Columbia" through modernity — would symbolically foreground the "virgin land" and its inevitable male conquest.[36] The implications of this transaction become obvious and familiar: its connection to the American myth of progress; its service, once the frontier was considered closed in 1893, of the Gospel of Wealth; and, as always, its invitation to violence.[37] Mary V. Dearborn has identified in American literary history, a staid tradition of encounters

---

33 Todorov, 48-49, 58, 246.
34 Kolodny, 4.
35 Ibid., 6.
36 Ibid., 5, 6, 30; for a more detailed exploration of "Columbia" and early American literature, see Frank J. Cavaioli, "Columbus and the Rise of American Literature."
37 Kolodny, 67, 133, 22.

between symbolic European male John Rolfes and ethnically Other female Pocahontases—particularly in literature that foregrounds questions of national and/or ethnic identity.[38] It would seem that when the John Rolfe is himself ethnic, then Pocahontas, in order to embody more contemporarily what is thought to be native, becomes decidedly more American. Just as Annette Kolodny views Jay Gatsby's pursuit of Daisy Buchanan as a modern recurrence of Virgin Land mythology, so may we view Gennaro Accuci's pursuit of American(ized) women.[39] Jay Gatsby (née Gatz) may very well be Jewish— at the very least, his pseudonym renders him ethnically suspect— while Daisy is of Irish extraction and, by 1920s standards, unimpeachably American. Similarly, Gennaro's ultimate romantic conquest is the more assimilated and savvy Carmela Dauri. Gennaro Accuci, in his sexual exploits, proves he has the "aggressive temperament" thought necessary of an immigrant male on the make, particularly as this was understood for Italian-American men, who drew upon ancient traditions of chivalry in order to define their relation to the public and private spheres.[40]

When he brutishly claims housekeeper Zia Nuora as his own, it becomes difficult for him to imagine sending for Rosaria and his family. Smarter, prettier, and— unlike Gennaro's hopelessly untutored, Old World wife—exhibiting the cosmopolitan, more easily Americanized manner of a Northern Italian, Gennaro views Nuora as more than a lover:

> To lie in her arms at night, the men sleeping in the other rooms, not daring to whisper what they knew, fed his ego, proved his vast success in America! End it all! No, by the saints. And yet in

---

38 Dearborn, 3-11.
39 Kolodny, 138.
40 Shumsky, 206; Gardaphé, *From Wiseguys to Wisemen*, 15-20.

> some obscure animal way he knew he should love the woman at whose side he had slept from the day he was eighteen [. . .]. The heavy hours of toil with her, followed by the dark drowsy nights when they sought the soft of their bodies for easement and the sleep that would not flow into their exhausted work-drawn muscles — these hours came back in his scattered broodings about her. They seemed in a far-back time before the man he really was had emerged out of his strength, the new strength that cut down the halters that bound him to the life of a peasant-slave. (GG 24)

As the arrival of Gennaro's family nears, the reader is told that thoughts of his wife "disturbed him. They did more than disturb him. They angered him. She seemed the living proof of another life from which he had fled. He had come into new ways and into new thoughts, and she would be filled with the old notions" (GG 92). Indeed, her Old World otherness is rendered physically in her lack of sexual desirability. When she arrives, Gennaro "found it impossible to say a word to her. She seemed so different with her Italian shoes, her laced bodice, her swinging skirts, her hair, braided and wound around her head, her skin burned with sun despite the long voyage" (GG 95). As Werner Sollors has demonstrated, American literature of consent (one's willed actions) and descent (one's ancestral culture), particularly ethnic literature, frequently associates Old and New World experience with love interests who come to embody one or the other.[41] *The Grand Gennaro* is no exception, so while Rosaria conjures up images of the protagonist's Old World, hardship-filled past of descent, Nuora reminds him of the freedom and success he has found in his New World life of consent. Gennaro himself makes the connection for Nuora: "'I was not like this, ever' he said. 'Only my wife before this. No other woman. There's something

---

41 Sollors, 149-73.

grown up in me, a madness, I don't know, ever since I saw the farm in the old country going for taxes and falling always deeper in debt and no hope ahead, and I picked up without saying good-bye, owing everybody money. [. . .] I found this thing growing in me ever since my farm kept going from me for the taxes and the mortgages, etc. It's a strength but a bad strength. That's why when you laughed and you made jokes and you stood up with your fine body tall and strong, your hair like my wife's, the strength came" (*GG* 21-22). In other words, Gennaro's sexual prowess increases as he comes closer to living the New World life he seeks, and, time and time again, money and sex are textually conjoined to help drive home the point. When explaining to his peers why he chooses to stay in America, Gennaro says that it is not simply because "the women here are easy to get and the money is easy to make" (*GG* 38). More than notches on the proverbial bedpost, the women he so easily gets come closer to embodying the polar opposite of Rosaria, who, not being "a prize he had wrested [. . .] out of the air of a new environment," simply does not fit into his New World narrative (*GG* 98). He takes a liking to Dora Levin, the Americanized second-generation daughter of a Jewish pushcart salesman. When he brings her back to his house, unashamed of the scandal this will undoubtedly cause, the narrator tells us: "And here he was now, head of a holy society, house-owner, a big business in hands, commanding the women he wanted when he wanted, and no one saying him 'nay'" (*GG* 57). Next, he pursues and brings home a dancer named Miss Waterson, which, much to the chagrin of community moralists like Zia Anna and Don Anselmo, sets off a string of orgiastic house parties fit for a Roman conqueror. Lapolla's depictions of Gennaro's exploits veer toward the ironic when he is shown to be fallible.[42] Dora Levin sees other men, Miss Waterson calls him "an Eyetalian," and another dancer temporarily steals his earrings: all three women provoke him to animalistic violence (GG 68, 78, 87). As if to underscore the point, Lapolla later has Don Tomaso tearfully tell his wife Donna Sofia, "We've made America at last" when his daughter Carmela is raped by Gennaro's son Domenico, forcing the two into a temporary honor marriage that would have made the Dauri family "rich" (GG 138). Significantly, Gennaro is not allowed true happiness in love until he revises his stance toward assimilation, humanizes his business practices, and ceases to see women as material prizes to accumulate. Carmela, after her marriage is annulled at the suggestion of Protestant social workers and she is sent to boarding school, becomes a perfectly integrated second-generation Italian-American character, living and working among Italians but exhibiting all the qualities of the professionally and intellectually well-adjusted "new woman" described in works by Henry James, Kate Chopin, and Sarah Orne Jewett: "she spoke English so fluently, she went about with so much assurance and poise, she must certainly understand a good deal. She had been educated in the American way, dressed in the American way, held herself up in an unmistakable American way, easy, self-contained, always unembarrassed" (GG 199). "*Quella buona buona*" and "*l'Americana*," Carmela is transformed into the perfect mate —neither too Italian nor too American—for Gennaro, who is by then neither a *contadino* nor a conqueror (GG 257).

"Making America" also refers to Gennaro and immigrants of all varieties making and remaking the cultural and social

---

42   Marazzi, "King of Harlem," 202-3.

fabric of America, participating in the building of that storied "nation of nations" Walt Whitman celebrates in *Leaves of Grass* (1855). William Dean Howells declared in "Our Italian Assimilators: A Paper Read at the Annual Meeting of the New York Society for Italian Immigrants" (1909) that "it was not for us to assimilate [the Italians], but for them to assimilate us."[43] Early-twentieth-century proponents of both melting pot theory, such as Israel Zangwill (*The Melting Pot*, 1908), and cultural pluralism, such as Horace A. Kallen ("Democracy Versus the Melting-Pot: A Study of American Nationality," 1915) and Randolph S. Bourne (Trans-National America," 1916), though notably silent about non-European Americans, believed that European immigrants contributed to the variety, richness, and even the very sustainability of American culture. Meanwhile, Anglo-conformists and immigration restrictionists such as Madison Grant, whose *Passing of the Great Race* (1916) set the standard for intellectually sanctioned racism in the early-twentieth century, expressed anxiety about the so-called New Immigration, the wave of southern- and eastern-European migrants that arrived in the United States between 1880 and 1924 and its genetic assault on Anglo-Teutonic America, which was peopled by presumably superior migrants from northern and western Europe. The 1911 U. S. Immigration Commission, also known as the (Senator William P.) Dillingham Commission, drew heavily upon racialist theory and sociology in order to create a forty-two-volume report analyzing the racial aptitude of the many ethnic groups inhabiting the United States. Predictably, in the study, old immigrants are viewed as beneficial to America's civic and cultural health while new immigrants are viewed as destructive.

---

43   Howells, "Our Italian Assimilators," 28.

The findings of this report found their way into congressional debates that resulted in the Emergency Quota Act of 1921 and the Immigration Act of 1924, both of which stifled immigration from most countries thought to produce immigrants of a racial pedigree that rendered them unfit to participate in American democracy.[44] If Anglo-conformists, "melting potters," and cultural pluralists could agree on one thing, it was the immigrant's power to reenact the Mayflower voyage and remake America anew. Lapolla helps the reader visualize this process by describing the succession of ethnic groups inhabiting the neighborhood in which *The Grand Gennaro* is set, the historical narrative discourse giving the immigrants' cultural footprints the fixity of a *fait accompli*:

> In the decade beginning with 1880 the East River front in Harlem was a quiet near-suburban locality, prized for residences by German and Irish immigrants long enough in the country to have established prosperous businesses. A solid German butcher with dubious notions of architecture had bought himself a plot not too far from the river to afford himself the luxury of a view and had erected upon it an odd oblong of a house, and just below the cornice had had the name PARTERRE inscribed in huge brownstone letters. [. . .]. They are all gone, these houses, now—all but a few which some of the second generation Italians, following obscure artistic impulses, have attempted to restore. Into them rushed the peasants that had left their impoverished farms in Calabria or Sicily, in the Apuglie, or in Basilicata. Where one family lived, now five or six struggled for a bit of space for a bed and a chance at the only sink or water-closet. In the back-yards, goats disported; in the front-yards, shacks mushroomed—old boards covered with rusty tin, plastered with Sunday supplements. In the streets swarmed tribes of children, bare-footed and scantily clad, forever unwashed but always screeching with glee. (*GG* 3-4)

---

44 See Desmond King's *Making Americans: Immigration, Race, and the Origins of the Diverse Democracy*.

Indeed, as Robert Viscusi points out, *The Grand Gennaro* "shows Italianization and Americanization as parallel processes in the Italian Harlem of the 1890s."[45] In the aforementioned "Our Italian Assimilators," Howells describes a similar succession of immigration to New York—Dutch, English, Irish, German, Asian, Russian, Jewish, and Greek—and concludes, "In view of the past changes which we have survived, I should be the last to dread our Italianization, which seems the next change in order," a change for which Howells believed the United States would "be the better."[46] Thus, the "unsettled negotiations" Dennis Barone speaks of between conflicting cultural inheritances and social processes have a profound effect not only upon the ethnic American—the usual focus of such inquiry—but also upon America itself.[47]

Finally, "making America" reminds us of Garibaldi M. Lapolla's authorial gesture in writing his novels. Having undergone the "ethnic passage" of all writers who wish to move "out of immigrant confines into the larger world of letters," as Thomas J. Ferraro would have it, Lapolla was free to participate in the creation of a national literature as it debated, figured, and refigured just what it means to be an American.[48] The titling of the *The Grand Gennaro* is clearly a revision of F. Scott Fitzgerald's titling of *The Great Gatsby* (1925), a more canonically credentialed text, much as the plot of *The Grand Gennaro*, though less directly, rehearses that of *The Great Gatsby*. *The Grand Gennaro* can safely be viewed as an Italian-American revision of the classic work. This act of titular and thematic

---

45 Viscusi, "Italian American Literary History from the Discovery of America," 158.
46 Howells, "Our Italian Assimilators," 28.
47 Barone, 7.
48 Ferraro, *Ethnic Passages*, 8.

revision is analogous to the one performed by Ralph Ellison's *Invisible Man* (1952) on Richard Wright's *Black Boy* (1940), a line of influence brilliantly detailed by Henry Louis Gates, Jr., in *The Signifying Monkey: A Theory of African-American Literary Criticism* (1988).[49] Like Ellison, Lapolla revises an ethnically specific canon, the then brief tradition of Italian-American literature comprised of writers such as Antonio Arrighi (1837-1920), Constantine Panunzio (1884-1964), and Silvio Villa (1882-1927), at the very same time he contributes to the enrichment of the American literary tradition. However, as he infuses an American success story with literary *italianità* — an expression which, proposed by Anthony Julian Tamburri as a means to read Italian-American literary difference, can be viewed as a variation upon Gates's theory of African-American literary Signifyin(g) — Lapolla does more than build up a national literature.[50] Additionally, in his Italian-tinged signification, he challenges readers' understanding of America itself. If we accept, as does Robert Anthony Orsi in his analysis of the Madonna of Mount Carmel and Italian Harlem, that symbolism interacts with individuals to create community, we must accept the role, however small, of works like *The Grand Gennaro* in the construction of not only Italian-American, but also American, community.[51] As he "invents Italian America" through his writing, as Fred L. Gardaphé would word it, or as he "writes Italy across America," as Robert Viscusi would, Lapolla reminds readers of the immigrants' transformative effect upon American history and culture and, indeed, participates in this very process himself.[52] As he does

---

49 Gates, Jr., 106.
50 Ibid., chapters 2 and 3; Tamburri, *A Semiotic of Ethnicity*, 14.
51 Orsi, *The Madonna of 115th Street*, 188.
52 Gardaphé, *Leaving Little Italy*, 13-35; Viscusi, *Buried Caesars*, 86-90.

this, he revises received literary stereotypes of Italian Americans and provides a counter-narrative to mainstream literary representations of Italian ethnic difference.

In the late-nineteenth-century United States, the migratory influx of Southern and Eastern Europeans coincided with the heyday of a literary genre ostensibly equipped to describe the place of these newcomers in the national scene. At least as its primary theorist and practitioner William Dean Howells saw it, realism was in part an attempt to broaden America's understanding of itself through the literary representation of the many ethnic and regional traditions that comprised the national culture.[53] According to Howells, if the realist kept a sensitive eye open to the cultural diversity that seemed increasingly to define the modern United States, then the result would be twofold: a literature that was distinctly American and a literature that could act as a potential impetus for social change. A native Ohioan of solid Anglo stock, Howells wrote a number of works that serve as a testament to the seeming inevitability of the realist's encounter and engagement with "the Other" in both non-fiction and fiction. The results, however, for Howells and others, are neither entirely unproblematic nor universally productive when their authorial gaze turned to their new Italian fellow citizens.

If we take Howells, Henry James, and Mark Twain to be the "big three" of American realism and briefly examine their treatment of Italian characters, we find that these authors don't always live up to the highest standards of mimetic accuracy. In fact, with regards to Italian Americans, two representative, and polar opposite, types seem to emerge: the ro-

---

53 On William Dean Howells and ethnic authorship, see Robert M. Dowling, "Ethnic Realism," particularly 360-1.

manticized Italian and the barbaric Italian.[54] In Twain's *Those Extraordinary Twins* (1894), two Italian twins named Luigi and Angelo Cappello are scheduled to arrive at Dawson Landing, Missouri, much to the amazed admiration of the locals. "It's so romantic!" exclaims Rowena Cooper in giddy anticipation of their arrival. "Just think—there's never been one in this town, and everybody will want to see them, and they're all *ours*! Think of that!"[55] When the two do finally arrive, the reader finds they are not the run-of-the-mill, unlearned southern Italians that comprised the bulk of Italian immigration, but, rather, two culturally conversant, well-dressed, and ultimately romanticized Italian gentlemen. Of course, it doesn't help that Luigi and Angelo are actually a two-headed monster. And while the Missourians' response to the strange "Eyetalians" is given a consciously ironic treatment, the fact remains that Twain's venture into representing the Italian "other" resulted in two characters that are anything but realistic. This tendency to romanticize the Italian is also found in Howells's *A Foregone Conclusion* (1875), whose protagonist, the priest Don Ipollito, is educated, completely well-spoken, and utterly unlike the Italians Howells encountered during his editorial tenures in both Boston and New York.

As is well known, Henry James's treatment of Italians isn't nearly as kind, and it comes to exemplify the stereotype of the barbaric, brutish immigrant. More candidly bigoted than Twain or Howells would ever dream of being, James left the United States as an adult because of its presumed cultural and social inadequacies. Upon his temporary return from 1904 to

---

54 See John Paul Russo's "From Italophobia to Italophilia: Representations of Italian Americans in the Early Gilded Age" and Joseph P. Cosco's *Imagining Italians: The Clash of Romance and Race in American Perceptions, 1880-1910*.
55 Twain, *Pudd'nhead Wilson* and *Those Extraordinary Twins*, 123.

1905, James observed and catalogued the changing cultural landscape of the United States, and he viewed much of it with distaste and alarm in his 1907 account *The American Scene*. James's own professed goal as a realist was to lend his writings "the air of reality."[56] And while his motivation, unlike Howells, was more aesthetic than social, he clearly committed himself to a high standard of representational verisimilitude. Did he live up to it in his depictions of Italian immigrants? Arguably, no, and the grotesque characteristics they begin to embody reveal more about his own cultural anxieties than the immigrants he purports to describe. Writing about his visit to New York City, James voices concern over the entry of "foreign matter into our heterogeneous system." The whole process of immigration and absorption becomes for James a process of "ingurgitation on the part of our body politic" and nothing short of a "free assault" upon America.[57] To James, the Italian becomes not only a subject of mystery—particularly regarding their eventual assimilation into the American social fabric—but also a target of condescension in his occasional encounters with them.

James's cultural anxiety in *The American Scene* has been well-documented, and it becomes a point of departure for studies like William Boelhower's *Immigrant Autobiography in the United States* and Delia Caparoso Konzett's *Ethnic Modernisms*. But the literary grotesqueries it produces, taken collectively with Twain's and Howells's own representational difficulties, point us toward a central problem of American literary realism: that biases, prejudices, and standards of decency chafe at the realist's veneer of mimetic objectivity and cause the whole project of realism to be, in many ways,

---

56   James, "The Art of Fiction," 53.
57   James, *The American Scene*, 50, 66, 67.

self-defeating. In other words, the socially constructed complex of ideas the realist brings to any text ultimately limits how realistic the author can be. This idea isn't new and has been generously explored in studies like Amy Kaplan's *The Social Construction of American Realism* (1988) and Michael Davitt Bell's *The Problem of American Realism* (1993). But the implications of this paradox of the unreal realist are more profound: that is, if there is a limit to the representational goal of American realism, then there is likely also a limit its sociopolitical goal, at least as Howells viewed it. And rather than figure the realist text as a utopian arena where the diverse peoples of the United States may join in common understanding, the realist may, by importing into his or her writing received notions of racial and ethnic difference, reify barriers between those very people. Elsa Nettels has examined how this is done linguistically in *Language, Race, and Social Class in Howells's America* (1988). Kenneth W. Warren comes to a similar conclusion in *Black and White Strangers: Race and American Literary Realism*: that despite the sociopolitical and aesthetic promise of realism, Howells, James, and others like them reinforced, rather than destroyed, barriers between the peoples of the United States and left us, at the end of the day, little better than "black and white strangers."

While this judgment may indeed be bleak, its implications need not be. To be sure, mainstream realists used the rhetorical appeal and the seeming transparency of their genre to generate an image of Italian Americans that was, wittingly or unwittingly, skewed by cultural biases and anything but realistic. However, it could also be argued that the earliest Italian-American writers, who generally were engaged with the idea of realistically representing Italian-American life, a "dislodging and debunking of negative stereotypes," as Anthony Julian Tamburri phrases it, brought to the texts they crafted their own biases, which were assuredly not the same as those of their "mainstream" literary counterparts.[58] Rather than reduce the Italian American to a one-dimensional stereotype, early Italian-American writers engage in the decidedly realist project of accurately describing Italian-American subjectivity in all of its complexity, possibility, and humanity: "establish[ing] a repertoire of signs, at times *sui generis*, [. . .] creat[ing] verbal variations [. . .] of what can be perceived as the Italian/American *interpretant*."[59] The result can be described as an Italian-American literary counter-narrative that dialogues with dominant narratives of Italian-American subjectivity and therein serves as both a response and a potential corrective: a "confirmation," "variation," "negation," or "substitution" of "codes" "of the dominant culture."[60] Although William Boelhower developed this four-part taxonomy to describe the rhetoric of Italian-American autobiography, I believe it is possible to extend this observation to most of the Italian-American literature published in the first half of the twentieth century.

In making this claim, I am assuredly *not* attempting to pigeonhole all of early Italian-American literary production into the rubric of realism. I am not unaware of the full range of narrative and poetic techniques deployed by these early writers. However, I would say that insofar as early Italian-American literature exhibits a commitment to mimetic accuracy, it engages in a realist endeavor, even as it is capable of a variety of techniques and devices to convey this accuracy. And, in advancing this theory, I am not attempting to marginalize

---
58   Tamburri, *A Semiotic of Ethnicity*, 4.
59   Ibid., 8.
60   Boelhower, 20.

the aesthetic components of the relevant works. I would suggest, however, that as with any ethnic American literary tradition—and the broader American literary tradition, for that matter—we find the earliest writers are preoccupied first with "telling the truth" before any artistic liberty is considered.

Realism is a good lens through which to view the emergence of Italian-American literature, particularly when we consider the editorial career of William Dean Howells. Writing for both the *Atlantic Monthly* and *Harper's Monthly* during the last three decades of the nineteenth century, Howells relentlessly campaigned for realism and argued in favor of the ethics of realistic description. As previously stated, Howells viewed realism as both a proponent for social change, as well as a literary showcase for multiethnic, multiregional America. Toward this noble end, he published and favorably reviewed regionalists like Sarah Orne Jewett and Bret Harte; "mainstream" realists like James and Twain; and "ethnic" realists such as Abraham Cahan and Charles Chesnutt. It is arguably with Abraham Cahan that we witness the birth of the Jewish-American novel in *Yekl* (1896) and *The Rise of David Levinsky* (1917), both of which, incidentally, bear a remarkable resemblance to *The Grand Gennaro*. And while I am unaware of any direct lineage between Howells and Italian-American writers, it seems to me that the earliest of them were preoccupied with accomplishing through literature something Howells would have appreciated, even if he couldn't always do it himself: that is, accurately describing the lives, dreams, and hardships of Italian Americans and adding their voice to the nation's literary landscape.

By the 1920s, American readers were certainly ready for this. In *The Harlem Renaissance in Black and White* (1995), George Hutchinson describes a national readership that craved "white ethnic" and African/American literature, and the influential New York publishers were more than willing to supply it. Over the first two decades of the twentieth century, the ameliorative influence of cultural pluralist intellectuals like Josiah Royce, Horace Kallen, and Randolph Bourne came to fruition in the increasingly popular ethnic- and African-American literature of the 1920s. And Hutchinson sees both white ethnic and Harlem Renaissance literature as sharing a number of motivations that sound to this author a great deal like Howells's. For example, Hutchinson writes that "The Harlem Renaissance program of using the arts to advance freedom and equality derived [. . .] from a belief in the central role of aesthetic experience, in the achievement of new forms of solidarity and understanding, and thus in the transformation and national integration of cultures."[61] Contemporary critics, such as H. L. Mencken, celebrated ethnic literature for its realism. And even though he cruelly dismissed Howells as a prudish Victorian, Mencken campaigned for ethnic literature on Howells's very terms. As Hutchinson writes, "With its almost ethnographic focus on cultural particularity, regional critical realism of the kind Mencken was encouraging privileged the 'indigenous' and the vernacular. Thus American culture as a whole began to emerge as a quiltlike complex of regional and ethnic cultures."[62]

Even when written during a time of high modernism, the abiding social realism of this era's immigrant fiction is striking. For Italian-American writers, the realist mode would predominate well into the 1930s and 40s, and it would neither be unnoticed nor unappreciated by indigenous critics. For example, in his 1935 and 1939 reviews of *The Grand Genna-*

---
61   Hutchinson, 90.
62   Ibid., 317.

ro and *Christ in Concrete*, Jerre Mangione praises both works on the grounds of their realism, the former, as we have seen, for its "Italo-Americans who are vivid and alive" (rather than the one-dimensional stereotypes provided by contemporary gangster movies) and the latter for its "genuine feeling about Italians . . . working and living together."[63] To be sure, if one thing binds most early Italian-American literature—from the modernist immediacy of Arturo Giovannitti's *Arrows in the Gale* (1914) to the romantically tinged realism of Giuseppe Cautela's *Moon Harvest* (1925) to the more thoroughgoing realism of Louis Forgione's *Reamer Lou* (1924) to the doubly gripping naturalism and modernism of di Donato's *Christ in Concrete* (1939)—there is a common desire to fill in literary absences: something Howells would have celebrated had he lived long enough to read about it.[64]

However, Italian-American counter-narrative is capable of correcting not only misleading dominant narratives but indigenous ones, as well. It has been often convincingly argued that Italian-American male writers from di Donato to Puzo have had a tendency to romanticize the Italian-American woman as a perennially submissive, pious, and domestic, if also strong, being. Scholars such as Rose Basile Green and Helen Barolini have noted that this trend was not reversed until Italian-American women began crafting their own fictions and giving three-dimensional life to Italian-American female subjectivity. This is a counter-realistic process that arguably begins with Mari Tomasi's *Like Lesser Gods* (1949) and continues in the 1960s with works like Octavia Waldo's *A Cup of the Sun* (1961) and Marion Benasutti's *No Steadyjob for*

---

63 Mangione, Review of *The Grand Gennaro*, 313; Mangione, "Little Italy," 111.
64 For a discussion of Howells in the context of Italian-American literature, see Scambray, 10-14.

Papa (1966). In each case, to some degree, realistic accuracy strikes a blow against romanticized inaccuracy, those "emblematic types and scenarios" Joseph Sciorra describes "that trigger immediate and ingrained assumptions about people's beliefs, politics, aesthetics, values, and behaviors that leave little room for nuance and elaboration."[65] Realism arguably has been a means for Italian-American literature to move beyond what Anthony J. Tamburri describes as "a series of reminiscences that lead primarily to recall" — a problem that occasionally plagues not only Italian-American literature but Italian-American studies on the whole. Ideally, the realist project then becomes a means by which "to revisit our past, reclaim its pros and cons, and reconcile it with our present."[66]

These days, the Italian-American writer has a full arsenal of literary techniques, modes, themes, and tropes at his or her disposal. The works of Tony Ardizzone, Tina DeRosa, Helen Barolini, Rose Romano, Rachel Guido DeVries, and many others, are ample evidence of this. Some remain steeped in ethnic tradition; others avoid it completely. Still others alternate between the two. Some, such as Giose Rimanelli in *Benedetta in Guysterland*, favor a postmodern literary discourse that riffs on the Italian-American literary tradition and parodizes its traditional commitment to historical accuracy. However, in even a text as seemingly radical as Rimanelli's, there is a felt need on the part of the reader to reflect back to the earlier, more realistically consistent representatives of the Italian-American literary canon in order to understand it. It would seem that this continual experimentation with representational possibility is the motivating factor behind any vital literary tradition. However, what should never be forgotten is the fact that if, in

---

65   Sciorra, 2.
66   Tamburri, *Re-reading Italian Americana*, 19.

these supposedly post-ethnic times, Italian-American authors have the luxury to take certain liberties — to exercise a "postmodern prerogative" as Fred L. Gardaphé terms it — it is because of the efforts of those who preceded them and devoted much of their literary energy to "setting the record straight" and thereby creating Italian-American literature.[67]

---

[67] Gardaphé, *Italian Signs*, 153.

Note: GMLP = MSS 64, Garibaldi M. Lapolla Papers, Historical Society of Pennsylvania, Philadelphia.

Bibliography

Aaron, Daniel. "The Hyphenate Writer and American Letters." *Smith Alumnae Quarterly* (July 1964): 213-17.

Achebe, Chinua. "The Novelist as Teacher." 1965. In *An Anthology of Criticism and Theory*, eds. Tejumola Olaniyan and Ato Quayson, 103-6. Maiden, MA: Blackwell, 2007.

Adler, Mortimer J. *Philosopher at Large: An Intellectual Autobiography*. New York: Macmillan Publishing Co., 1977.

Alba, Richard D. *Italian Americans: Into the Twilight of Ethnicity*. Englewood Cliffs, NJ: Prentice-Hall, Inc., 1985.

Albright, Carol Bonomo. "Literature." In *The Italian American Experience: An Encyclopedia*, eds. Salvatore J. LaGumina, Frank J. Cavaioli, Salvatore Primeggia, and Joseph A. Varacalli, 342-8. New York: Garland Publishing, 2000.

Albright, Carol Bonomo, and Christine Palamidessi Moore, eds. *American Woman, Italian Style: Italian Americana's Best Writings on Women*. New York: Fordham University Press, 2011.

"America's Interest in the Education of Italian Children." In *The Italians: Social Backgrounds of an American Group*, eds. Francesco Cordasco and Eugene Bucchioni, 483-87. Clifton, NJ: Augustus M. Kelley Publishers, 1974.

Amfitheatrof, Erik. *The Children of Columbus: An Informal History of the Italians in the New World*. Boston: Little, Brown and Company, 1973.

Ancestry.com. Accessed 28 March, 2015. http://search.ancestry.com/cgi-bin/sse.dll?rank=1&new=1&MSAV=0&msT=1&gss=angs-g&gsfn=garibalde&gsln=lapolla&mswpn=1652382&mswpn_PInfo=6-%7c%7c1652393%7c0%7c2%7c%7c3244%7c35CATEGORY&h=2210235&recoff=8+10&db=NYCmarriageindexes&indiv=1&ml_rpos=2

Assistant Superintendent and the Principals of Districts Forty-three and Forty-four in the City of New York. "In Memoriam: Garibaldi M. Lapolla." GMLP, Box 1, Folder 8.

Banfield, Edward C. *The Moral Basis of a Backward Society*. New York: The Free Press, 1958.

Barone, Dennis. *America/Trattabili*. New York: Bordighera Press, 2011.

Bayor, Ronald H. *Neighbors in Conflict: The Irish, Germans, Jews, and Italians of New York City, 1929-1941*. Urbana, IL: University of Illinois Press, 1988.

Bell, Michael Davitt. *The Problem of American Realism: Studies in the Cultural History of a Literary Idea*. Chicago: University of Chicago Press, 1993.

Benasutti, Marion. *No Steady Job for Papa*. New York: Vanguard, 1966.

Bersani, Leo. *The Freudian Body: Psychoanalysis and Art*. New York: Columbia University Press, 1986.

_____. *A Future for Astyanax: Character and Desire in Literature*. Boston: Little, Brown and Company, 1976.

Bersani, Leo and Ulysse Dutoit. *The Forms of Violence: Narrative in Assyrian Art and Modern Culture*. New York: Schocken Books, 1985.

Birnbaum, Michele. *Race, Work, and Desire in American Literature, 1860-1930*. Cambridge, England: Cambridge University Press, 2003.

Blackburn, Marc K. "Register of the Garibaldi Mario Lapolla Papers, 1930-1976, MSS. Group 64." GMLP.

Boelhower, William. *Immigrant Autobiography in the United States: Four Versions of the Italian American Self*. Verona: Essedue Edizioni, 1982.

Bona, Mary Jo. *By the Breath of Their Mouths: Narratives of Resistance in Italian America*. Albany, NY: State University of New York Press, 2010.

Bourne, Randolph. "Trans-National America." In *Theories of Ethnicity: A Classical Reader*, ed. Werner Sollors, 93-108. New York: Oxford University Press, 1996.

Bove, Aldo, and Giuseppe Massara. *'Merica: A Conference on the Culture and Literature of Italians in North America*. January 2003, Rome and Cassino, Italy. Stony Brook, NY: Forum Italicum, 2006.

Brooks, Peter. *Reading for the Plot: Design and Intention in Narrative.* New York: Alfred A. Knopf, 1984.

Brown, Mary Elizabeth. "Covello, Leonard (1887-1982)." In *The Italian American Experience: An Encyclopedia*, eds. Salvatore J. Lagumina, Frank J. Cavaioli, Salvatore Primeggia, and Joseph A. Varacalli, 149-50. New York: Garland Publishing, Inc., 2000.

Bryant, Dorothy. *Miss Giardino.* 1978. Rprt., New York: The Feminist Press at the City University of New York, 1997.

Burke, Edmund. *A Philosophical Enquiry into the Origin of Our Ideas of the Sublime and Beautiful.* 1757. Rprt., London: Routledge and Kegan Paul, 1958.

Butler, Judith. "Desire." In *Critical Terms for Literary Study*, eds. Frank Lentricchia and Thomas McLaughlin, 369-86. Chicago: University of Chicago Press, 1995.

Cahan, Abraham. *The Rise of David Levinsky.* 1917. Rprt. New York: Penguin Books, 1993.

_____. Yekl *and* The Imported Bridegroom *and Other Stories of Yiddish New York.* 1896, 1898. Rprt. New York: Dover, 1970.

Cautela, Giuseppe. *Moon Harvest.* New York: The Dial Press, 1925.

Cavaioli, Frank J. "Columbus and the Rise of American Literature." In *New Explorations in Italian American Studies*, eds. Richard N. Juliani and Sandra P. Juliani, 3-17. November 1992, Washington, DC. Staten Island, New York: American Italian Historical Association, 1994.

Clayton, Jay. "Narrative and Theories of Desire." *Critical Inquiry* 16.1 (Autumn 1989): 33-53.

Cordasco, Francesco, and Eugene Bucchino, eds. *The Italians: Social Backgrounds of an American Group.* Clifton, NJ: Augustus M. Kelley Publishers, 1974.

Cosco, Joseph P. *Imagining Italians: The Clash of Romance and Race in American Perceptions, 1880-1910.* Albany, New York: State University of New York, 2003.

Covello, Leonard. *The Social Background of the Italo-American School Child: A Study of the Southern Italian Family Mores and Their Effect on the School Situation in Italy and America.* 1967. Rprt., Totowa, NJ: Rowman and Littlefield, 1972.

Covello, Leonard, with Guido d'Agostino. *The Heart Is the Teacher: The Teacher in the Urban Community*. 1958. Rprt., Totowa, NJ: Littlefield, Adams, and Company, 1970.

Covin, David. "Henry Dumas: The Writer as Teacher." *Black American Literature Forum* 22:2 (Summer 1988): 202-5.

Dearborn, Mary V. *Pocahontas's Daughters: Gender and Ethnicity in American Culture*. New York: Oxford University Press, 1986.

de Conde, Alexander. *Half Bitter, Half Sweet: An Excursion into Italian-American History*. New York: Charles Scribner's Sons, 1971.

de Lauretis, Teresa. *Alice Doesn't: Feminism, Semiotics, Cinema*. Bloomington, Ind.: Indiana University Press, 1984.

Deleuze, Gilles and Félix Guattari. *Anti-Oedipus: Capitalism and Schizophrenia*. Minneapolis: University of Minnesota Press, 1983.

Den Tandt, Christopher. *The Urban Sublime in American Literary Naturalism*. Urbana, Ill.: University of Illinois Press, 1998.

Dewey, John. *Democracy and Education*. 1916. Rprt., New York: The Free Press, 1966.

di Donato, Pietro. *Christ in Concrete*. Indianapolis: Bobbs-Merrill Company, 1939.

Dowling, Robert M. "Ethnic Realism." In *A Companion to American Fiction 1865-1914*, eds. Robert Paul Lamb and G. R. Thompson, 356-76. Malden, Mass.: Blackwell Publishing, 2005.

"Editor's Notebook." *Sunday Herald*, June 21, 1953. Newspaper clipping. Box 4, folder 12, GMLP.

Egelman, William S. "Education: Sociohistorical Background." In *The Italian American Experience: An Encyclopedia*, eds. Salvatore J. Lagumina, Frank J. Cavaioli, Salvatore Primeggia, and Joseph A. Varacalli, 193-98. New York: Garland Publishing, Inc., 2000.

"Extracts from Reviews of *The Grand Gennaro*." GMLP, box 3, folder 1.

Feld, Rose. "'Making America' in Little Italy." Review of *The Grand Gennaro*, by Garibaldi M. Lapolla. *New York Herald Tribune Books*, September 1, 1935, 4.

Ferraro, Thomas. *Ethnic Passages: Literary Immigrants in Twentieth-Century America*. Chicago: University of Chicago Press, 1993.

_____. "Ethnicity and the Marketplace." In *The Columbia History of the American Novel*, ed. Emory Elliott, 380-406. New York: Columbia University Press, 1991.

_____. *Feeling Italian: The Art of Ethnicity in America*. New York: New York University, 2005.

Fiedler, Leslie. *Love and Death in the American Novel*. New York: Stein and Day, 1966.

Foerster, Robert F. *The Italian Emigration of Our Times*. Cambridge, MA: Harvard University Press, 1919.

Forgione, Louis. *Reamer Lou*. New York: E. P. Dutton, 1924.

Foster, Dennis A. *Sublime Enjoyment: On the Perverse Motive in American Literature*. Cambridge, England: Cambridge University Press, 1997.

Foucault, Michel. *The History of Sexuality, Volume I: An Introduction*. 1976. Trans. Robert Hurley. Rprt., New York: Vintage Books, 1980.

_____. *The History of Sexuality, Volume II: The Use of Pleasure*. 1984. Trans. Robert Hurley. Rprt., New York: Pantheon Books, 1985.

Freud, Sigmund. *Beyond the Pleasure Principle*. 1920. Trans and ed. James Strachey. Rprt., New York: W. W. Norton, 1961.

_____. *Civilization and Its Discontents*. 1930. Trans. and ed. James Strachey. Rprt., New York: W. W. Norton, 1961.

Gabaccia, Donna R. *From Sicily to Elizabeth Street: Housing and Social Change among Italian Immigrants, 1880-1930*. Albany, NY: State University of New York Press, 1984.

Gallo, Patrick J. *Ethnic Alienation: The Italian-Americans*. Rutherford, NJ: Fairleigh Dickinson University Press, 1974.

_____. *Old Bread, New Wine: A Portrait of the Italian-Americans*. Chicago: Nelson-Hall, 1981.

Gambino, Richard. *Blood of My Blood: The Dilemma of the Italian Americans*. 1974. Rprt., Toronto: Guernica, 1996.

Gans, Herbert J. *The Urban Villagers: Group and Class in the Life of Italian-Americans*. New York: The Free Press, 1962.

Gardaphé, Fred L. *From Wiseguys to Wisemen: The Gangster and Italian American Masculinities*. New York: Routledge, 2006.

———. *Italian Signs, American Streets: The Evolution of Italian American Narrative*. Durham, North Carolina: Duke University Press, 1996.

———. *Leaving Little Italy: Essaying Italian American Culture*. Albany, New York: State University of New York Press, 2004.

Garrett-Petts, W. F. "Novelist as Radical Pedagogue: George Bowering and Postmodern Reading Strategies." *College English* 54:5 (September 1992): 554-72.

Gates, Henry Louis, Jr. *The Signifying Monkey: A Theory of African-American Literary Criticism*. New York: Oxford University Press, 1988.

Gill, Jonathan. *Harlem: The Four Hundred Year History from Dutch Village to Capital of Black America*. New York: Grove Press, 2011.

Giovannitti, Arturo. *Arrows in the Gale*. Riverside, Connecticut: Hillacre Bookhouse, 1914.

Girard, René. *Deceit, Desire, and the Novel: Self and Other in Literary Structure*. Baltimore: The Johns Hopkins Press, 1965.

Girgus, Sam. *Desire and the Political Unconscious in American Literature: Eros and Ideology*. New York: St. Martin's Press, 1990.

Giunta, Edvige. *Writing with an Accent: Contemporary Italian American Women Writers*. New York: Palgrave, 2002.

Glazer, Nathan, and Daniel P. Moynihan. *Beyond the Melting Pot: The Negroes, Puerto Ricans, Jews, Italians, and Irish of New York City*. 2nd ed. Cambridge, MA: The M.I.T. Press, 1970.

Golding, Alan. "From Pound to Olson: The Avant-Garde Poet as Pedagogue." *Journal of Modern Literature* 34.1 (Fall 2010): 86-106.

Goodheart, Eugene. *Desire and Its Discontents*. New York: Columbia University Press, 1991.

Grant, Madison. *The Passing of the Great Race or the Racial Basis of European History*. Revised ed. New York: Charles Scribner's Sons, 1919.

Green, Rose Basile. *The Italian-American Novel: A Document of the Interaction of Two Cultures*. Rutherford, N.J.: Fairleigh Dickinson University Press, 1974.

Greven, David. *Men Beyond Desire: Manhood, Sex, and Violation in American Literature.* New York: Palgrave Macmillan, 2005.

Gurock, Jeffrey S. *When Harlem Was Jewish, 1870-1930.* New York: Columbia University Press, 1979.

Hawthorne, Nathaniel. *The Scarlet Letter.* 1850. Rprt., New York: Penguin Books, 1986.

Hofstadter, Richard. *Social Darwinism in American Thought.* Revised ed. Boston: The Beacon Press, 1955.

Hornsby, Robert. E-mail to the author. October 2, 2007.

Howells, William Dean. *A Foregone Conclusion.* 1875. Rprt. in *Novels 1875-1886: A Foregone Conclusion, A Modern Instance, Indian Summer, The Rise of Silas Lapham.* New York: Library of America, 1982.

_____. "Our Italian Assimilators: A Paper Read at the Annual Meeting of the New York Society for Italian Immigrants." *Harper's Weekly,* April 10, 1909, 28.

_____. *The Rise of Silas Lapham.* 1885. Rpt. New York: Penguin Classics, 1986.

Hutchinson, George. *The Harlem Renaissance in Black and White.* Cambridge, Mass.: The Belknap Press of Harvard University Press, 1995.

Iannone, Carol. "Leonard Covello: Teaching Immigrants in the American Way." *Italian Americana* 20.1 (Winter 2002): 36-47.

Iorizzo, Luciano J. and Salvatore Mondello. *The Italian Americans.* Boston: Twayne Publishers, 1980.

Jakobson, Roman. "Two Aspects of Language and Two Types of Aphasic Disturbances." In *Fundamentals of Language,* eds. Morris Halle and Roman Jakobson, 53-82. The Hague: Mouton, 1956.

James, Henry. *The American Scene.* 1907. Rprt. New York: Penguin Books, 1994.

_____. "The Art of Fiction." 1884. Rprt. in *Henry James: Essays on Literature American Writers, English Writers,* ed. Leon Edel, 44-65. New York: Library of America, 1984.

Jameson, Fredric. *The Political Unconscious: Narrative as a Socially Symbolic Act.* Ithaca, N.Y.: Cornell University Press, 1981.

Johanek, Michael C. and John L. Puckett. *Leonard Covello and the Making of Benjamin Franklin High School: Education As If Citizenship Mattered*. Philadelphia: Temple University Press, 2007.

Kallen, Horace M. "Democracy Versus the Melting-Pot: A Study of American Nationality." In *Theories of Ethnicity: A Classical Reader*, ed. Werner Sollors, 67-92. New York: New York University Press, 1996.

Kant, Immanuel. *The Critique of Judgement*. 1790. Trans. James Creed Meredith. Rprt. in *The Critique of Pure Reason, The Critique of Practical Reason and Other Ethical Treatises, and The Critique of Judgement*, Great Books of the Western World, ed. Robert Maynard Hutchins, vol. 42, 459-613. Chicago: Encyclopedia Britannica, 1952.

Kaplan, Amy. *The Social Construction of American Realism*. Chicago: University of Chicago Press, 1988.

Kessner, Thomas. *The Golden Door: Italian and Jewish Immigrant Mobility in New York City, 1880-1915*. New York: Oxford University Press, 1977.

King, Desmond. *Making Americans: Immigration, Race, and the Origins of the Diverse Democracy*. Cambridge, Mass.: Harvard University Press, 2000.

Kolodny, Annette. *The Lay of the Land: Metaphor as Experience and History in American Life and Letters*. Chapel Hill, North Carolina: University of North Carolina Press, 1975.

Konzett, Delia Caparoso. *Ethnic Modernisms: Anzia Yezierska, Zora Neale Hurston, Jean Rhys, and the Aesthetics of Dislocation*. New York: Palgrave MacMillan, 2002.

Kristeva, Julia. *Desire in Language: A Semiotic Approach to Literature and Art*, ed. Leon S. Roudiez, trans. Thomas Gora, Alice Jardine, and Leon S. Roudiez. New York: Columbia University Press, 1980.

Lacan, Jacques. *Écrtis: A Selection*, trans. Alan Sheridan. New York: W. W. Norton, 1977.

Lagumina, Salvatore J., Frank J. Cavaioli, Salvatore Primeggia, and Joseph A. Varacalli, eds. *The Italian American Experience: An Encyclopedia*. New York: Garland Publishing, Inc., 2000.

Lapolla, Garibaldi M. "The American Novel." Box 2, folder 3, GMLP.

_____. "Are Our Public Schools So Bad?" Box 1, folder 13, GMLP.

_____. *Better High School English through Tests and Drills*. New York: Noble and Noble, 1929.

_____. Brooklyn, to Leonard Covello, Bronx, October 22, 1930. MSS 40, box 99, folder 2, transcript. Leonard Covello Papers, Historical Society of Pennsylvania, Philadelphia.

_____. European Trip Diary. 1953. GMLP, Box 1, Folder 9.

_____. *The Fire in the Flesh*. New York: The Vanguard Press, 1931; rprt., New York: Arno Press, 1975.

_____. *The Grand Gennaro*. New York: The Vanguard Press, 1935; rprt., New York: Arno Press, 1975.

_____. *Italian Food for the American Kitchen*. New York: Wilfred Funk, 1953.

_____. "Letter in Answer to Dr. Lefkowitz about So-Called Communist Teachers." GMLP, Box 1, Folder 2, 3-5.

_____. *Miss Rollins in Love*. New York: The Vanguard Press, 1932.

_____. *The Mushroom Cook Book*. New York: Wilfred Funk, 1953.

_____. "On the East River: Midnight." 1951. GMLP, box 7, folder 5.

_____. "Principles of Modern Educational Procedures." GMLP, Box 1, Folder 11.

_____. *Required Grammar in the New York Public Schools*. New York: Noble and Noble, 1937.

_____. Returned letter. New York, to Mark O. Lapolla, December 25, 1944. GMLP, box 1, folder 3.

_____. Returned letter. New York, to Mark O. Lapolla, January 7, 1945. GMLP, box 1, folder 3.

_____. Returned letter. New York, to Mark O. Lapolla, January 15, 1945. GMLP, box 1, folder 3.

_____. Returned letter. New York, to Mark O. Lapolla, January 31, 1945. GMLP, box 1, folder 3.

_____. Returned letter. New York, to Mark O. Lapolla, February 6, 1945. GMLP, box 1, folder 3.

———. "Shelley and the Political Parties of His Day." M.A. thesis, Columbia University, 1911.

———. Untitled ink and pen drawing. GMLP, box 6, folder 4.

———. Untitled pen sketch. 1951. GMLP, box 5, folder 10.

———. Untitled pencil sketch. GMLP, box 6, folder 7.

———. Untitled watercolor. GMLP, box 7, folder 4.

———. Untitled watercolor. GMLP, box 7, folder 5.

Lapolla, Paul. Telephone interview. June 25, 2007.

———. Telephone interview. October 3, 2007.

———. Telephone interview. November 11, 2007.

Lapomarda, Vincent A. "Higher Education." In *The Italian American Experience: An Encyclopedia*, eds. Salvatore J. Lagumina, Frank J. Cavaioli, Salvatore Primeggia, and Joseph A. Varacalli, 285-87. New York: Garland Publishing, Inc., 2000.

La Sorte, Michael. *La Merica: Images of Italian American Greenhorn Experience*. Philadelphia: Temple University Press, 1985.

Lear, Paul. E-mail to the author. October 1, 2007.

Limerick, Patricia Nelson. *The Legacy of Conquest: The Unbroken Past of the American West*. New York: W. W. Norton and Company, 1987.

Lopreato, Joseph. *Italian Americans*. New York: Random House, 1970.

Lord, Eliot, John J. D. Trenor, and Samuel J. Barrows. *The Italian in America*. New York: B. F. Buck and Company, 1905.

Luisa, Maria. "Le Conversazioni del Giovedì." *Il Progresso Italo-Americano*, April 2, 1953, 1.

Malpezzi, Frances M. and William M. Clements. *Italian-American Folklore*. Little Rock, Ark.: August House Publishers, 1992.

Mangano, Antonio. *Sons of Italy: A Social and Religious Study of the Italians in America*. New York: Missionary Education Movement of the United States and Canada, 1917.

Mangione, Jerre. "Little Italy." Review of *Christ in Concrete*, by Pietro di Donato. *New Republic*, August 30, 1939, 111-12.

———. Review of *The Grand Gennaro*, by Garibaldi M. Lapolla. New Republic, October 23, 1935, 313.

Mangione, Jerre, and Ben Morreale. *La Storia: Five Centuries of the Italian American Experience*. New York: HarperCollins, 1992.

Marazzi, Martino. "I Due Re di Harlem." *Belfagor* 58.5 (Sept. 2003): 533-49.

———. "King of Harlem: Garibaldi Lapolla and Gennaro Accuci 'Il Grande.'" In *'Merica: A Conference on the Culture and Literature of Italians in North America*, eds. Aldo Bove and Giuseppe Massara, 190-210. Jan. 2003, Rome and Cassino, Italy. Stony Brook, NY: Forum Italicum, 2005.

Mariano, John Horace. *The Second Generation of Italians in New York City*. Boston: The Christopher Publishing House, 1921.

Marsh, Fried T. Review of *The Grand Gennaro*, by Garibaldi M. Lapolla. In "'The Grand Gennaro' and Some Other Recent Works of Fiction." *New York Times*, September 1, 1935, BR6.

Meckel, Richard A. "A Reconsideration: The Not So Fundamental Sociology of Garibaldi Marto Lapolla." *MELUS* 3:4 (1987): 127-39.

Miller, James. "The Novelist as Teacher: Chinua Achebe's Literature for Children." *Children's Literature* 9 (1981): 7-18.

"Missing Flight Officer Now Is Reported Killed." *New York Times*, January 6, 1946, 30.

Mitchell, Lee Clark. *Determined Fictions: American Literary Naturalism*. New York: Columbia University Press, 1989.

Mulas, Francesco. *Studies on Italian-American Literature*. New York: Center for Migration Studies, 1995.

Musmanno, Michael A. *The Story of the Italians in America*. Garden City, NY: Doubleday and Company, Inc., 1965.

Nelli, Humbert S. *From Immigrants to Ethnics: The Italian Americans*. Oxford, England: Oxford University Press, 1983.

Nettels, Elsa. *Language, Race, and Social Class in Howells's America*. Lexington, Ky.: University Press of Kentucky, 1988.

New York Times, January 1954, 29.

Oesterreicher, Anna N. "Recollections of Gari Lapolla." GMLP, Box 1, Folder 8.

Oliver, Lawrence J. "'Beyond Ethnicity': Portraits of the Italian-American Artist in Garibaldi Lapolla's Novels." *American Studies* 28:2 (1987): 5-21.

———. "'Great Equalizer' or 'Cruel Stepmother'?: Image of the School in Italian-American Literature." *The Journal of Ethnic Studies* 15:2 (1987): 113-30.

———. "The Re-Visioning of New York's Little Italies: From Howells to Puzo." *Multi-Ethnic Literatures of the Americas* 14:3/4 (Autumn-Winter 1987): 5-22.

Ontario Post. September 22, 1917.

———. September 29, 1917.

———. December 8, 1917.

———. April 20, 1918.

———. May 25, 1918.

———. June 1, 1918.

Orsi, Robert Anthony. "The Fault of Memory: 'Southern Italy' in the Imagination of Immigrants and the Lives of Their Children in Italian Harlem, 1920-1945." *Journal of Family History* 15:2 (1990): 133-47.

———. *The Madonna of 115th Street: Faith and Community in Italian Harlem, 1880-1950.* New Haven, Conn.: Yale University Press, 1985.

Osofsky, Gilbert. *Harlem: The Making of a Ghetto.* Second Edition. Chicago: Elephant Paperbacks, 1971.

Pari-Pfisterer, Caroline. "Divided Worlds: Autobiographical Literacy Narratives and Italian-American Women Writers." VIA 22:1 (Spring 2011): 3-20.

Parrino, Maria. "Education in the Autobiographies of Four Italian Women Immigrants." In *American Woman, Italian Style: Italian Americana's Best Writings on Women*, eds. Carol Bonomo Albright and Christine Palamidessi Moore, 55-77. New York: Fordham University Press, 2011.

Patri, Angelo. *A Schoolmaster of the Great City: A Progressive Educator's Pioneering Vision for Urban Schools.* 1917. Rprt., New York: The New Press, 2007.

Peebles, Robert Whitney. *Leonard Covello: A Study of an Immigrant's Contribution to New York City.* 1967. Rprt., New York: Arno Press, 1978.

Peragallo, Olga. *Italian-American Authors and Their Contribution to American Literature*, ed. Anita Peragallo. New York: S. F. Vanni, 1949.

Perrone, Vito. *Teacher with a Heart: Reflections on Leonard Covello and Community*. New York: Teachers College Press, 1998.

Pisani, Lawrence Frank. *The Italian in America: A Social Study and History*. New York: Exposition Press, 1957.

Prezzolini, Giuseppe. "*Stati Uniti: autobiografia e romanzo*." *Gazzetta del Popolo*, December 19, 1934.

"Principals Lose Pay Case." *New York Times*, June 2, 1950, 12.

P.S. 174 Faculty. "In Memoriam: Garibaldi M. Lapolla: Friend, Educator, Humanitarian." GMLP, Box 1, Folder 8.

Rabinowitz, Paula. *Labor and Desire: Women's Revolutionary Fiction in Depression America*. Chapel Hill, N.C.: The University of North Carolina Press, 1991.

Review of *The Fire in the Flesh*, by Garibaldi M. Lapolla. "'The Blind Man' and Other Recent Works of Fiction." *New York Times*, April 12, 1931, BR4.

Review of *The Grand Gennaro*, by Garibaldi M. Lapolla. *Boston Transcript*, December 18, 1935, 3.

Review of *The Grand Gennaro*, by Garibaldi M. Lapolla. *Saturday Review of Literature* 12 (October 1935): 28, 30.

Review of *Miss Rollins in Love*, by Garibaldi M. Lapolla. In "'Call Home the Heart' and Other Works of Fiction." *New York Times*, February 28, 1932, BR7.

Rimanelli, Giose. *Benedetta in Guysterland*. Montreal: Guernica, 1993.

Rolle, Andrew. *The American Italians: Their History and Culture*. Belmont, CA: Wadsworth Publishing Company, 1972.

_____. *The Immigrant Upraised: Italian Adventurers and Colonists in an Expanding America*. Norman, OK: University of Oklahoma, 1968.

_____. *The Italian Americans: Troubled Roots*. New York: The Free Press, 1980.

Rose, Philip M. *The Italians in America*. New York: George H. Doran Company, 1922.

Russo, John Paul. "From Italophilia to Italophobia: Representations of Italian Americans in the Early Gilded Age." *Differentia* 6-7 (Spring/Autumn 1994): 45-75.

Sampson, Harriet. "Winy Folks." Review of *The Fire in the Flesh*, by Garibaldi M. Lapolla. *New York Herald Tribune Books*, April 5, 1931, 16.

Scambray, Kenneth. *The North American Italian Renaissance: Italian Writing in America and Canada*. Toronto: Guernica, 2000.

Schiavo, Giovanni. *Four Centuries of Italian-American History*. 4th ed. 1957. Rprt., Staten Island, NY: Center for Migration Studies of New York, Inc., 1992.

_____. *Italian-American History, Volume I*. New York: The Vigo Press, 1947.

_____. *Italian-American History, Vol. II : The Italian Contribution to the Catholic Church in America*. 1949. Rprt., New York: Arno Press, 1975.

Schiavone, James. *God from Afar: Memoirs of a University Professor*. San Jose: toExcel Press, 2000.

"A Schoolmarm in Love." Review of *Miss Rollins in Love*, by Garibaldi M. Lapolla. *New York Times*, February 28, 1932, 21.

Sciorra, Joseph. "Introduction: Listening with an Accent." *Italian Folk: Vernacular Culture in Italian-American Lives*, ed. Joseph Sciorra, 1-10. New York: Fordham UP, 2011.

Sedgwick, Eve Kosofsky. *Between Men: English Literature and Male Homosocial Desire*. New York: Columbia University Press, 1985.

See, Fred G. *Desire and the Sign: Nineteenth-Century American Fiction*. Baton Rouge, La.: Louisiana State University Press, 1987.

Sexton, Patricia Cayo. *Spanish Harlem: Anatomy of Poverty*. New York: Harper Colophon Books, 1966.

Shumsky, Neil Larry. "Return Migration in American Novels of the 1920s and 1930s." In *Writing Across Worlds: Literature and Migration*, eds. Russell King, John Connell, and Paul White, 198-215. New York: Routledge, 1995.

Sinclair, Upton. *The Goslings: A Study of the American Schools*. Pasadena, CA: Upton Sinclair, 1924.

Smith, Henry Nash. *Virgin Land: The American West as Symbol and Myth*. Cambridge, MA: Harvard UP, 1950.

Sollors, Werner. *Beyond Ethnicity: Consent and Descent in American Culture*. New York: Oxford University Press, 1986.

Tamburri, Anthony Julian. *Re-reading Italian Americana: Specificities and Generalities on Literature and Criticism*. Madison, NJ: Fairleigh Dickinson UP, 2014.

_____. *A Semiotic of Ethnicity: In (Re)cognition of the Italian/American Writer*. Albany, NY: State University of New York Press, 1998.

Tate, Claudia. *Domestic Allegories of Political Desire: The Black Heroine's Text at the Turn of the Century*. New York: Oxford University Press, 1992.

_____. *Psychoanalysis and Black Novels: Desire and the Protocols of Race*. New York: Oxford University Press, 1998.

"Teachers Oppose Loss of Royalties." *New York Times*, September 17, 1946, 7.

"Teachers Secretly Quizzed on Loyalty." *New York Times*, May 17, 1922, 18.

Thomas, Norman, et al. Letter to the editor. *The New Republic*, May 26, 1917, 109-11.

Todaro, Mary. Review of *The Fire in the Flesh*, by Garibaldi Marto Lapolla. April 21, 1932. Transcript. MSS 40, box 99, folder 2. Leonard Covello Papers, Historical Society of Pennsylvania, Philadelphia.

Todorov, Tzvetan. *The Conquest of America: The Question of the Other*, trans. Richard Howard. Norman, Oklahoma: University of Oklahoma Press, 1999.

Tomasi, Mari. *Like Lesser Gods*. 1949. Rprt. Shelburne, Vermont: The New England Press, 1988.

Tricarico, Donald. *The Italians of Greenwich Village*. Staten Island, NY: Center for Migration Studies, 1984.

Tripathi, P. D. "Is There a Moral in These Tales? (And What Is It Then?): An Appraisal of Chinua Achebe as Novelist Teacher." In *The African Fiction*, ed. Shyam S. Agarwalla, 105-23. New Dehli, India: Prestige, 2000.

Twain, Mark. *Pudd'nhead Wilson* and *Those Extraordinary Twins*. 1894. Rprt. New York: W. W. Norton, 1980.

Van Doren, Mark, and Garibaldi M. Lapolla, eds. *Junior Anthology of World Poetry*. New York: Charles and Albert Boni, 1929.

Viscusi, Robert. *Buried Caesars and Other Secrets of Italian American Writing*. Albany, New York: State University of New York Press, 2006.

_____. "Debate in the Dark: Love in Italian-American Fiction." In *American Declarations of Love*, ed. Ann Massa, 155-73. New York: St. Martin's Press, 1990.

_____. "Italian American Literary History from the Discovery of America." In *The Italian American Heritage: A Companion to Literature and Arts*, ed. Pellegrino d'Acierno, 151-64. New York: Garland Publishing, Inc., 1999.

_____. "Making Italy Little." In *Social Pluralism and Literary History: The Literature Of Italian Emigration*, ed. Francesco Loriggio, 61-90. Toronto: Guernica, 1966.

Waldo, Octavia. *A Cup of the Sun*. New York: Harcourt, 1961.

Wallace, James M. *The Promise of Progressivism: Angelo Patri and Urban Education*. New York: Peter Lang, 2006.

Warren, Kenneth W. *Black and White Strangers: Race and American Literary Realism*. Chicago: University of Chicago Press, 1993.

Weiskel, Thomas. *The Romantic Sublime: Studies in the Structure and Psychology of Transcendence*. Baltimore: The John Hopkins University Press, 1976.

Weyler, Karen A. *Intricate Relations: Sexual and Economic Desire in American Fiction, 1789-1814*. Iowa City, Iowa: University of Iowa Press, 2004.

Whitman, Walt. *Leaves of Grass*. 1855. Rprt. New York: Penguin Books, 2005.

Whittaker, David. "The Novelist as Teacher: *Things Fall Apart* and the Hauntology of Chimanda Ngozi Adichie's *Half of a Yellow Sun*." *Chinua Achebe's* Things Fall Apart, *1958-2008*, ed. David Whittaker, 107-17. Amsterdam, Netherlands: Rodopi, 2011.

Whyte, William Foote. *Street Corner Society: The Social Structure of an Italian Slum*. 4th ed. Chicago: U of Chicago P, 1993.

Workers of the Federal Writers' Project, Works Progress Administration. *The Italians of New York*. 1938. Rprt., New York: Arno Press, 1969.

Zandy, Janet. "Afterword: 'Teaching Was My Work.'" In *Miss Giardino*, by Dorothy Bryant, 161-85. 1978. Rprt., New York: The Feminist Press at the City University of New York, 1997.

Zangwill, Israel. *The Melting-Pot Drama in Four Acts*. Revised ed. New York: The MacMillan Company, 1915.

Index

Aaron, Daniel, xxv
accent, xxvi–xxvii
Achebe, Chinua, 72–73
Adler, Mortimer, xii
Advisory Council on the Qualification of Teachers, xiv
Agnese (*Fire in the Flesh*)
    acquisitiveness of, 5
    compared to Hester Prynne, 38
    eroticism and, 8, 10–11
    money and, 9, 10–11
    power of, 6, 8–9, 12–13
    religiosity and, 15–16
    transcendent and, 31–32
Albright, Carol Bonomo, 80, 81
"American fever," 87
American realism, 37–38
American Scene, The (James), 101
Americanization, 46, 50, 57, 82, 94. see also "making America"
Anglo-conformists, 95–96
Ardizzone, Tony, xxv
"Are Our Public Schools So Bad?" (Lapolla), 62
Arrows in the Gale (Giovannitti), 106
art
    Achebe on, 72
    in *The Fire in the Flesh*, 26–27, 30, 32, 34–35
    Lapolla's, 29–30, 40–42
    in *Miss Rollins in Love*, 66, 67–68
assimilation, 77–78, 81–82, 95, 97. see also Americanization; "making America"

Barolini, Helen, xxv, 106
Barone, Dennis, 97
Bell, Michael Davitt, 102
Benasutti, Marion, 106–107
Benedetta in Guysterland (Rimanelli), 107
Benjamin Franklin High School, 59–60
Better High School English (Lapolla), xv, 62–63
Birnbaum, Michele, 8
Black and White Strangers (Warren), 102
Black Boy (Wright), 98
Boelhower, William, 101, 103
Bona, Mary Jo, xxvii
Bourne, Randolph S., 95
Bread Givers (Yezierska), 88
Brooks, Peter, 6
brownstones, 10
Buck, Pearl, xviii
Buried Caesars and Other Secrets of Italian American Writing (Viscusi), xxvii
Burke, Edmund, 28
By the Breath of Their Mouths (Bona), xxvii

cactus metaphor, 70–71
Cahan, Abraham, 104
campanilismo, xxii
Cautela, Giuseppe, 106

"Children's Problems" column (Patri), 54
Christ in Concrete (di Donato), 83, 106
Circolo Italiano, Il (The Italian Circle), 58–59
Clements, William M., 15
Columbia University, xii
community school, 53, 54
conquest, 88–91
conscientious objectors, xiv
Coppino Law (1877), 44, 45
Cosenza, Mario, 59
Covello, Leonard, xiii, 37, 43, 49, 57–61, 64, 74, 75
Covin, David, 74
cultural pluralism, 60, 95, 96, 105
Cup of the Sun, A (Waldo), 106
"Custom-House, The" (Hawthorne), 37

de Lauretis, Teresa, 13
Dearborn, Mary V., 90–91
death instincts (Thanatos), 2
"Debate in the Dark" (Viscusi), 8
Democracy and Education (Dewey), 51
Den Tandt, Christophe, 29
desire
    attempted description of, 23–24
    concept of, 2–4
    destruction and, 24–26
    fire imagery and, 16–19
    resistance and, 21–22
    violence and, 19–20
Dewey, John, xiv, 44, 49–53, 54, 55, 60–62, 64, 75
DeWitt Clinton High School, xii, xiii, 58–59

di Donato, Pietro, 83, 106
Dillingham Commission, 95–96
domus, xx–xxi
Dumas, Henry, 74

education
    Covello and, 57–61
    Dewey and, 49–53
    Italian Americans and, 43–49
    Lapolla and, 61–63
    novel writing and, 71–76
    Patri and, 53–57
Ellison, Ralph, 98
Emergency Quota Act (1921), 96
Emerson, Ralph Waldo, 29
ethical idealism, xix n21
"Ethical Principles Underlying Education" (Dewey), 55
ethnic literature, Hutchinson on, 105
Ethnic Modernisms (Konzett), 101

Feld, Rose, 79, 84
Ferraro, Thomas J., xi, 29, 80, 88, 97
Fiedler, Leslie, 13
Fire in the Flesh, The (Lapolla)
    art and, 26–27, 30, 32, 34–36
    in-betweenness and, 30–33
    business plot of, 5, 9–11
    concept of desire and, 2–4, 6
    Covello and, 74
    family plot of, 6–8
    fire imagery in, 16–18, 21, 23, 25, 37
    grotesques in, 20–21, 25–26
    love plot of, 5, 8–9
    Mafia in, xxi
    power and, 12–15
    publication of, 1
    realism in, 35–37
    reception of, 1–2
    resistance and, 21–23

The Scarlet Letter and, 37–38
  synopsis of, 4–6
  transcendent and, 15–16, 18, 26–29
  violence and, 7–8, 19, 24, 25
Fitzgerald, F. Scott, 97
Foregone Conclusion, A (Howells), 100
Forgione, Louis, 106
forgiveness, 15
Fort Ontario, xii–xiii
Freud, Sigmund, 27

Gallo, Patrick J., 47
Gambino, Richard, 48
Gardaphé, Fred L., xxiv, xxv–xxvi, 80, 98, 108
gardening symbolism, 70–71, 76
Garrett-Petts, W. F., 73
Gates, Henry Louis, Jr., 98
gender
  in Italian-American literature, 106–107
  power and, 12–13
G.I. Bill, 49
Giardino, Anna, 75–76
Gill, Jonathan, xxii
Giovanni (*Fire in the Flesh*)
  art of, 26–27, 30, 32, 34–35
  binaries and, 4
  as Christ figure, 30
  familial love and, 6–7
  transcendent and, 16
Giovannitti, Arturo, 106
Girard, René, 35
Giunta, Edvige, xxvi–xxvii
God from Afar (Schiavone), 76
Godfather, The (Puzo), 88
Golding, Alan, 73

Gospel of Wealth, 90
Grand Gennaro, The (Lapolla)
  assimilation in, 77–78, 81–82, 97
  The Fire in the Flesh and, 2
  friendship in, 81
  history of Harlem in, 74
  Mafia in, xxi
  "making America" in, 82–88, 94–95
  reception of, 79–81
  reviews of, 105–106
  sexual themes and, 88–94
  synopsis of, 77–79
Grant, Madison, 95
Great Gatsby, The (Fitzgerald), 91, 97
Green, Rose Basile, xxiii–xxiv, 2, 65, 80, 81, 106
Greven, David, 13
grotesques, 20–21, 25–26
Gualdo, Giovanni, 46

hands-on learning, 51, 74–75
Harlem Renaissance in Black and White, The (Hutchinson), 104–105
Hawthorne, Nathaniel, 37–38
Heart is the Teacher, The (Covello), 59, 75
House Un-American Activities Committee, xv
Howells, William Dean, 38, 95, 97, 99–100, 102, 104–106
Hutchinson, George, 104–105
"Hyphenate Writer and American Letters, The" (Aaron), xxv

Iannone, Carol, 60
identity, 33
Immigrant Autobiography in the United States (Boelhower), 101
Immigration Act (1924), 96

immigration restrictionists, 95–96
in-betweenness, 30–35, 39
insatiability, 2, 26–27, 30
insularity, xxii
Invisible Man (Ellison), 98
Italian Americans, stereotypes of, 99–101, 102–103
Italian Cooking for the American Kitchen (Lapolla), xv, xvi, 75
Italian Harlem, xx–xxii
Italian Signs, American Streets (Gardaphé), xxiv
Italian-American Authors and Their Contribution to American Literature (Peragallo), 1–2, 80
Italian-American literary context, xxiii–xxviii
Italian-American Novel, The (Green), xxiii, 80
italianità (Italianness), xxv, 4, 98

Jakobson, Roman, 36
James, Henry, 99, 100–101
"Jerry" (Lapolla), xv
Joint Legislative Committee to Investigate Seditious Activities (Lusk Committee), xiv
Junior Anthology of World Poetry, The (Van Doren and Lapolla), xv

Kallen, Horace A., 95
Kant, Immanuel, 28
Kaplan, Amy, 102
Kolodny, Annette, 90
Konzett, Delia Caparoso, 101
Kosofsky Sedgwick, Eve, 13

Language, Race, and Social Class in Howells's America (Nettels), 102
Lapolla, Garibaldi M. *see also individual works*
  aesthetic approach of, xvii–xix
  biography of, xii–xvii
  cookbooks of, 74–75
  Covello and, 58
  education and, 49–50, 61–63, 71–76
  Italian Harlem domus and, xx–xxii
  Italian-American literary context for, xxiii–xxviii
  lack of critical attention to, xi
  "making America" and, 98
Lapolla, Margaret (neé McCormick), xiii
Lapolla, Mark Oreste, xiii, xvi–xvii
Lapolla, Paul McCormick, xiii
Lapolla, Priscilla (neé Sherman), xiii, xvii
Lay of the Land, The (Kolodny), 90
Leaves of Grass (Whitman), 95
life instincts (Eros), 2
Like Lesser Gods (Tomasi), 106
literacy rates, in Italy, 44–45
literary naturalist style, 24
Lusk Committee (Joint Legislative Committee to Investigate Seditious Activities), xiv

Madonna of 115th Street, The (Orsi), xx
Mafia/organized crime, xxi, 14–15
"making America," 9–10, 77, 82–88, 94–95, 97. *see also* Americanization
Malpezzi, Frances M., 15
Mangano, Antonio, 50, 82

Mangione, Jerre, 79-80, 106
Marazzi, Martino, 2, 65, 80, 86
Marcontonio, Vito, 59
Mariano, John Horace, 51, 54
Marsh, Fred T., 79, 89
McMurray, Frank, 55
Meckel, Richard A., xviii n20, 80
Mencken, H. L., 105
Michele (*Fire in the Flesh*), power and, 12, 14
Miller, James, 72
Miss Giardino (Giardino), 75-76
Miss Rollins in Love (Lapolla)
    cactus metaphor in, 70-71
    love plot of, 68-69
    Mafia in, xxi
    reception of, 63
    state of public education and, 43
    synopsis of, 63-65
    views on education in, 65-68, 69-70, 75
Mitchell, Lee Clark, 24
moneymaking, 3, 9, 10-11, 20, 21
Montessori, Maria, 57
Moon Harvest (Cautela), 106
Mulas, Francesco, 28
Murillo, Bartolomé Esteban, 34
Mushroom Cookbook, The (Lapolla), xv, 74-75

need, desire and, 2-3
Nettels, Elsa, 102
No Steadyjob for Papa (Benasutti), 106-107
Norris, Frank, 38-39
novelist, as progressive educator, 71-76

"Novelist as Teacher, The" (Achebe), 72

Old World versus New World, 78, 88, 92-93. *see also* Americanization; "making America"
Oliver, Lawrence J.
    Dewey and, 50
    on *The Fire in the Flesh*, 2, 34
    on Italian-American literature, xviii n20, 33, 34
    on Lapolla's pedagogical views, 65, 69-70
    on *Miss Rollins in Love*, 67-68, 80
    on "romances of commonplace," xix n21, 38
Olson, Charles, 73
"On the East River: Midnight" (Lapolla), 30
Ontario Post, xiii
organized crime/Mafia, xxi, 14-15
Orsi, Robert Anthony, xx-xxi, 15, 80-81, 83, 98
"Our Italian Assimilators" (Howells), 95, 97

Pari-Pfisterer, Caroline, 68
Parrino, Maria, 68
passing narratives, 82
Passing of the Great Race (Grant), 95
Patri, Angelo, 49, 53-57, 59, 64, 70-71, 75
Peirce, Charles, xxv
Peragallo, Olga, 1-2, 63, 80
Pocahontas, 90
postmodernism, 73, 107, 108
Pound, Ezra, 73

power
    desire for, 12–14
    in *The Fire in the Flesh*, 6, 8–9, 12–15
    gender and, 12–13
"Principles of Modern Educational Procedures" (Lapolla), 61
Problem of American Realism, The (Bell), 102
Public School 112, xiii
Public School 174, xiii, xv, xvii
Puglia, James, 46
Pugliese, Anthony, 59
Puzo, Mario, 88

Rabinowitz, Paul, 14
racism, 95–96
realism, 4, 34, 39, 73, 99, 101–104, 105–106, 107
Reamer Lou (Forgione), 106
Required Grammar in the New York Public Schools (Lapolla), xv, 63
Rimanelli, Giose, 107
Rise of David Levinsky, The (Cahan), 104
Rise of Silas Lapham, The (Howells), 38
Rolfe, John, 90
romanticism, xviii–xix, 4, 8, 34, 36, 39, 73

Sampson, Harriet, 1
Scarlet Letter, The (Hawthorne), 37–38
Schoolmaster of the Great City, A (Patri), 54, 56, 70–71
Schiavone, James, 76
Sciorra, Joseph, xxvi–xxvii, 107
Semiotic of Ethnicity, A (Tamburri), xxv

Servicemen's Readjustment Act (1944), 49
settlement houses, 56
sex/eroticism
    in *The Fire in the Flesh*, 8, 10–11, 19
    in *The Grand Gennaro*, 88–94
    money and, 10–11
    violence and, 19
Shelley, Percy Bysshe, xii, xix
Shumsky, Neil Larry, 80
Signifying Monkey, The (Gates), 98
Sinclair, Upton, xiv
Smith, Henry Nash, 89
Social Background of the Italo-American School Child, The (Covello), 43, 75
Social Construction of American Realism, The (Kaplan), 102
Social Darwinism, 81
social justice, Lapolla's fights for, xiv–xv
Sollors, Werner, 92
Stella, Joseph, 29
stereotypes of Italian Americans, 99–101, 102–103
stuttering syntax, 23–24
sublime, 28–30, 31

Tamburri, Anthony Julian, xxv–xxvi, 98, 102–103, 107
Tate, Claudia, 13
Things Fall Apart (Achebe), 72
Thomas Jefferson High School, xiii
Those Extraordinary Times (Twain), 100
Todorov, Tzvetan, 89
Tomasi, Mari, 106

transcendent
    art and, 16, 26–29, 31–32
    desire for, 15–16
    fire imagery in, 18
Tripathi, P. D., 72
Twain, Mark, 99–100

urban sublime, 29–30

Van Doren, Mark, xv
Vico, Giambattista, xxiv
violence
    desire and, 19–20
    in *The Fire in the Flesh*, 7–8, 19, 24, 25
    moneymaking and, 20
    sex and, 19
Virgin Land (Smith), 89
Viscusi, Robert, xxii, xxvii, 8, 80, 83, 84, 86, 97, 98

Waldo, Octavia, 106
Warren, Kenneth W., 102
Whitman, Walt, 95
Whittaker, David, 73
work, as form of resistance, 21–22
World War I, xii–xiii, xiv
Wright, Richard, 98
Writing with an Accent (Giunta), xxvi

Yekl (Cahan), 104
Yezierska, Anzia, 88

Zandy, Janet, 76
Zangwill, Israel, 95

SAGGISTICA

Taking its name from the Italian—which means essays, essay writing, or non-fiction—*Saggisitca* is a referred book series dedicated to the study of all topics and cultural productions that fall under what we might consider that larger umbrella of all things Italian and Italian/American.

Vito Zagarrio
The "Un-Happy Ending": Re-viewing The Cinema of Frank Capra. 2011. ISBN 978-1-59954-005-4. Volume 1.

Paolo A. Giordano, Editor
The Hyphenate Writer and The Legacy of Exile. 2010. ISBN 978-1-59954-007-8. Volume 2.

Dennis Barone
America / Trattabili. 2011. ISBN 978-1-59954-018-4. Volume 3.

Fred L. Gardaphè
The Art of Reading Italian Americana. 2011. ISBN 978-1-59954-019-1. Volume 4.

Anthony Julian Tamburri
Re-viewing Italian Americana: Generalities and Specificities on Cinema. 2011. ISBN 978-1-59954-020-7. Volume 5.

Sheryl Lynn Postman
An Italian Writer's Journey through American Realities: Giose Rimanelli's English Novels. "The most tormented decade of America: the 60s" ISBN 978-1-59954-034-4. Volume 6.

Luigi Fontanella
Migrating Words: Italian Writers in the United States. 2012. ISBN 978-1-59954-041-2. Volume 7.

Peter Covino & Dennis Barone, Editors
Essays on Italian American Literature and Culture. 2012. ISBN 978-1-59954-035-1. Volume 8.

Gianfranco Viesti
Italy at the Crossroads. 2012. ISBN 978-1-59954-071-9. Volume 9.

Peter Carravetta, Editor
Discourse Boundary Creation (LOGOS TOPOS POIESIS): A Festschrift in Honor of Paolo Valesio. ISBN 978-1-59954-036-8. Volume 10.

Antonio Vitti and Anthony Julian Tamburri, Editors
Europe, Italy, and the Mediterranean. ISBN 978-1-59954-073-3. Volume 11.

Vincenzo Scotti
Pax Mafiosa or War: Twenty Years after the Palermo Massacres. 2012. ISBN 978-1-59954-074-0. Volume 12.

Anthony Julian Tamburri, Editor
Meditations on Identity. Meditazioni su identità. ISBN 978-1-59954-082-5. Volume 13.

Peter Carravetta, Editor
Theater of the Mind, Stage of History. A Festschrift in Honor of Mario Mignone. ISBN 978-1-59954-083-2. Volume 14.

Lorenzo Del Boca
Italy's Lies. Debunking History's Lies So That Italy Might Become A "Normal Country". ISBN 978-1-59954-084-9. Volume 15.

George Guida
Spectacles of Themselves. Essays in Italian American Popular Culture and Literature. ISBN 978-1-59954-090-0. Volume 16.

Antonio Vitti and Anthony Julian Tamburri, Editors
Mare Nostrum: prospettive di un dialogo tra alterità e mediterraneità. ISBN 978-1-59954-100-6. Volume 17.

Patrizia Salvetti
Rope and Soap. Lynchings of Italians in the United States. ISBN 978-1-59954-101-3. Volume 18.

Sheryl Lynn Postman and Anthony Julian Tamburri, Editors
Re-reading Rimanelli in America: Six Decades in the United States. ISBN 978-1-59954-102-0. Volume 19.

Pasquale Verdicchio
: *Bound by Distance. Rethinking Nationalism Through the Italian Diaspora.* ISBN 978-1-59954-103-7. Volume 20.

Peter Carravetta
: *After Identity. Migration, Critique, Italian American Culture.* ISBN 978-1-59954-072-6. Volume 21.

Antonio Vitti and Anthony Julian Tamburri, Editors
: *The Mediterranean As Seen by Insiders and Outsiders.* ISBN 978-1-59954-107-5. Volume 22.

Eugenio Ragni
: *After Identity. Migration, Critique, Italian American Culture.* ISBN 978-1-59954-109-9. Volume 23.

Quinto Antonelli
: *Intimate History of the Great War: Letters, Diaries, and Memoirs from Soldiers on the Front.* ISBN 978-1-59954-111-2. Volume 24.

Antonio Vitti and Anthony Julian Tamburri, Editors
: *The Mediterranean Dreamed and Lived by Insiders and Outsiders.* ISBN 978-1-59954-115-0. Volume 25.

www.ingramcontent.com/pod-product-compliance
Lightning Source LLC
Chambersburg PA
CBHW062107080426
42734CB00012B/2785